Year 4 Workbook

Published by Pearson Education Limited, 80 Strand, London, WC2R 0RL.
www.pearson.com/international-schools

Copies of official specifications for all Pearson Edexcel qualifications may be found on the website:
https://qualifications.pearson.com

Text © Pearson Education Limited 2022
Project managed and edited by Just Content Limited
Designed and typeset by PDQ Digital Media Solutions Limited
Picture research by SPi
Original illustrations © Pearson Education Limited 2022
Cover design © Pearson Education Limited 2022

The right of Jane Cotter to be identified as the author of this work has been asserted by her in accordance with the Copyright, Designs and Patents Act 1988.

First published 2022

24 23
10 9 8 7 6 5

British Library Cataloguing in Publication Data
A catalogue record for this book is available from the British Library

ISBN 978 1 292 39677 4

Printed and bound in Great Britain by Bell and Bain Ltd, Glasgow

Acknowledgements
The publisher would like to thank the following for their kind permission to reproduce their photographs:

Cover acknowledgements
Shutterstock: Janna7/Shutterstock 1

Text acknowledgements
Jacqueline Drye: Special child by Jacqueline Drye. Used with permission. 106; **Melissa & Doug:** Kieras, Julie. 5 Tips to Teach Kids How to Care for Plants. Melissa & Doug Blog. 68; **Nobel Prize Outreach AB:** Full Text of Alfred Nobel's Will. NobelPrize. org. 27 Sept. 2018 52; **Raising Children Network (Australia) Limited:** Community Activities: Getting Teenagers Involved. Raising Children Network, 10 Jan. 2019 126; **Save the Children (Sales) Limited:** Children's Rights. Save the Children UK 161; **The John Muir Trust:** Rewilding - an Introduction. Protecting and Repairing Wild Land 74; **The Woodland Trust:** Woodland Trust. Rewilding – the Woodland Trusts Position. Woodland Trust 73; **TheWorldCounts:** Sweatshop workers are paid as little as 3 cents per hour working up to 100+ hours a week in conditions of poor air quality and extreme heat. TheWorldCounts 134; **United Nations:** World Children's Day. United Nations 159; **Thomson Reuters:** Mills, Yasmin. Roma People: 10 Ways Europe's Biggest Minority Faces Discrimination. Reuters, Thomson Reuters, 8 Apr. 2019 26; **UNICEF:** Castle, Caroline, and John Burningham. For Every Child: the UN Convention on the Rights of the Child in Words and Pictures. Phyllis Folgelman, 2001 162; **UNITED NATIONS:** UN logo for Gender Equality. Goal 5 | Department of Economic and Social Affairs. UNITED NATIONS. Used with permission 29

Photos acknowledgements
123RF: Cathy Yeulet/123RF 103; ocusfocus/123rf.com 14; Cathy Yeulet/123RF 25; Wavebreak Media Ltd /123rf.com 130; meinzahn/123rf.com 159; jovannig/123rf.com 166; Kristina Bolgert. 123rf.com 14; **Alamy Stock Photo:** Trinity Mirror / Mirrorpix / Alamy Stock Photo 25; Jeff Morgan 09/Alamy Stock Photo 176; **Shutterstock:** jeff gynane/Shutterstock 25; chrisdorney/Shutterstock 25; Jeka/Shutterstock 45; Procy/Shutterstock 75; AB Photographie/Shutterstock 75; Szczepan Klejbuk/Shutterstock 75; Jerry Bouwmeester/Shutterstock 75; MilousSK/Shutterstock 11; Piyaset/Shutterstock 13; Atlaspix/Shutterstock 17; Yakovlev Sergey/Shutterstock 27; chinahbzyg/Shutterstock 28; wavebreakmedia/Shutterstock 46; VeronikaV/Shutterstock 52; a katz/Shutterstock 54; Innerspace Images/Shutterstock 60; David MacFarlane/Shutterstock 60; divedog/Shutterstock 60; blue-sea.cz/Shutterstock 60; Krakenimages.com/Shutterstock 60; Evlakhov Valeriy/Shutterstock 62; Stephen VanHorn/Shutterstock 69; Richard Peterson/Shutterstock 75; buteo/Shutterstock 75; Alexander-Glover/Shutterstock 111; neftali/Shutterstock 112; Rawpixel/Shutterstock 118; Evgeny Bakharev/Shutterstock 124; aapsky/Shutterstock 147; Anton_Ivanov/Shutterstock 182; steve estvanik/Shutterstock 182; YAKOBCHUK VIACHESLAV/Shutterstock 127; kwanchai.c/Shutterstock 44; **Getty Images:** Skynesher/Gettyimages 169; **Jules Selmes:** Jules Selmes/Pearson Education Ltd 17; **Tudor Photography:** Tudor Photography/Pearson Education Ltd 38

All other images © Pearson Education

Contents

Welcome to Global Citizenship!

We hope you will find this book useful as you approach the exciting subject of Global Citizenship! This book will form a key part of your journey to becoming a Global Citizen. It will help you understand the wider world, your place in it, how you can engage with issues locally and globally and how you can enact positive change.

Objective
This is what you will know or be able to do by the end of the session.

We will learn
This is what you will be learning in the session.

Key vocabulary
These are important words to know.

Information
This is an introduction to the session.

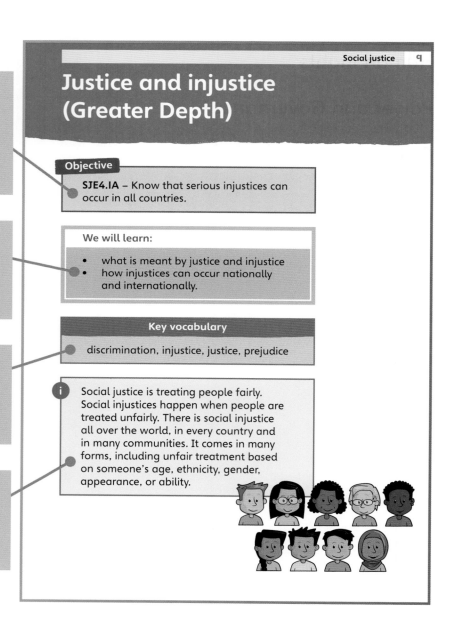

Social justice   9

Justice and injustice (Greater Depth)

Objective

SJE4.IA – Know that serious injustices can occur in all countries.

We will learn:

- what is meant by justice and injustice
- how injustices can occur nationally and internationally.

Key vocabulary

discrimination, injustice, justice, prejudice

Social justice is treating people fairly. Social injustices happen when people are treated unfairly. There is social injustice all over the world, in every country and in many communities. It comes in many forms, including unfair treatment based on someone's age, ethnicity, gender, appearance, or ability.

This book provides a clear structure to your learning. Each unit is based around a Global Citizenship strand and clearly focuses on the mastery of key objectives. These objectives are set out at the start of each session, along with the opportunity to reflect on what you have learned at the end of each session in the unit.

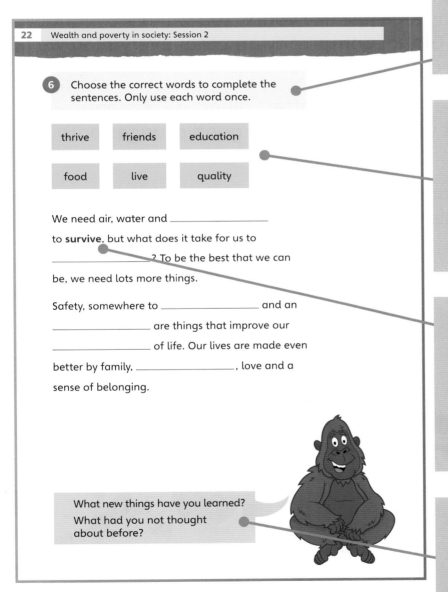

22   Wealth and poverty in society: Session 2

6   Choose the correct words to complete the sentences. Only use each word once.

| thrive | friends | education |
| food | live | quality |

We need air, water and _____ to **survive**, but what does it take for us to _____? To be the best that we can be, we need lots more things.

Safety, somewhere to _____ and an _____ are things that improve our _____ of life. Our lives are made even better by family, _____, love and a sense of belonging.

What new things have you learned? What had you not thought about before?

Instruction
Read this carefully to know what to do.

Activity
You might need to write or draw an answer, circle pictures or words, or tick or match answers.

Key vocabulary
Some tricky words are in **bold**. Find out what these mean in the Glossary at the back of the book.

You might have a question to think about, or discuss with a partner or adult.

Meet the mascots!

Global Citizens!

We are all part of a Global Community – we are Global Citizens!

In this book you will meet lots of different people. Some may seem to be like you and some may seem to be different. However, everyone you meet will have something in common with you! Some may be from a part of the world you know, or from a city, town or village just like yours. You will discover how we are all part of a Global Community and that everything we do has effects on people, animals, and the wider world.

You will find that the same issues affect all of us. This book will help you learn what you can do to make good changes both locally and globally.

You will also meet, and learn about, some of the different animals which are also facing problems and may need our help.

The Giant Panda

Giant Pandas now only live in China and are very rare. People are trying to protect their homes from destruction. Protecting their homes also helps a lot of other animals and provides them with somewhere to live.

The Malayan Tapir

Malayan Tapirs are found in parts of South-East Asia. Young tapirs are dark and have stripes to help them hide when they are little. Because of damage to their habitat they are endangered. Some groups are trying to protect them.

The Golden Jackal

Golden Jackals live in parts of Africa and are quite common. Because there are so many of them, they often meet people and can be found near houses and farms. We need to learn how to live safely alongside this animal.

The African Elephant

The African Elephant is the world's largest land animal and can weigh as much as three family cars! Over many years, they have often been hunted by poachers and by farmers trying to protect their land. Now people are learning about how to live alongside this giant.

The Sumatran Orangutan

The Sumatran Orangutan lives in the trees of tropical rainforests. The trees they live in are being cut down for wood and the land is used to grow other things which means they are very endangered. There are not many of these animals left now.

Justice and injustice (Greater Depth)

Objective

SJE4.IA – Know that serious injustices can occur in all countries.

We will learn:

- what is meant by justice and injustice
- how injustices can occur nationally and internationally.

Key vocabulary

discrimination, injustice, justice, prejudice

i Social justice is treating people fairly. Social injustices happen when people are treated unfairly. There is social injustice all over the world, in every country and in many communities. It comes in many forms, including unfair treatment based on someone's age, ethnicity, gender, appearance, or ability.

1 Circle those words below that might be used in relation to **prejudice** and **discrimination**.

understanding	judge	unfair	empathy

negative	fair	mistreat	positive

2 How can you avoid being prejudiced and discriminating against others? Tick all the strategies that will help you.

Make sure I have all the information before I make a judgement. ☐

Tell someone they can't play football because they are too short. ☐

Learn as much as I can about someone's background. ☐

Refuse to include someone in a game because of the way they look. ☐

Get to know a person before deciding if I will be their friend. ☐

Don't think all teachers are the same. ☐

List other strategies that might help you.

_____

_____

_____

3 What does **justice** mean? Why it is important? Write your thoughts below.

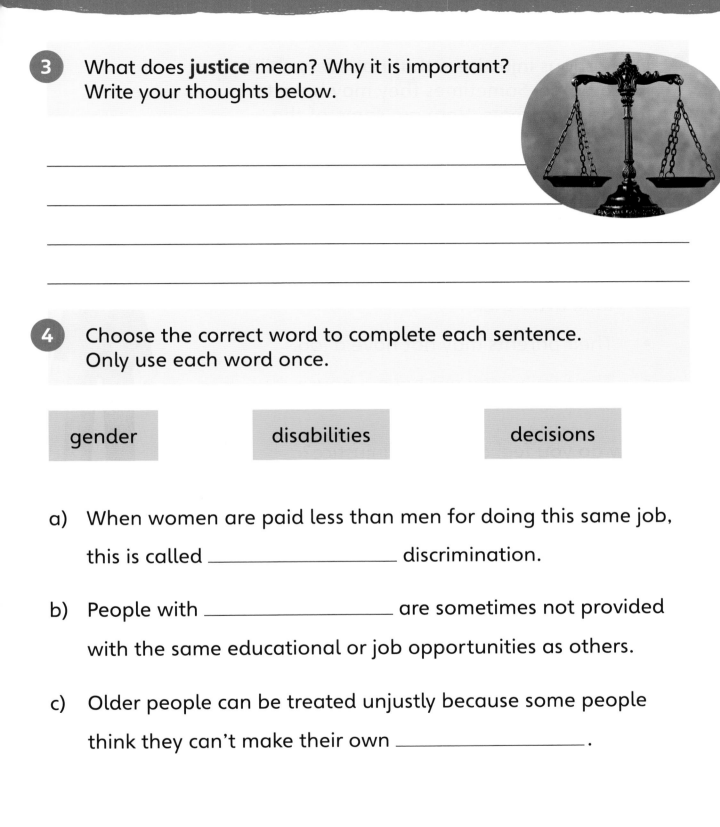

_____

_____

_____

_____

4 Choose the correct word to complete each sentence. Only use each word once.

| gender | disabilities | decisions |

a) When women are paid less than men for doing this same job, this is called _____ discrimination.

b) People with _____ are sometimes not provided with the same educational or job opportunities as others.

c) Older people can be treated unjustly because some people think they can't make their own _____ .

5 One serious injustice is that not every child has a home. Sometimes they may have to live on the streets. Here are some of the reasons why this may happen.

- They may not have a responsible adult to look after them.

- They may have to work on the streets.

- Their parents may be ill and unable to look after them.

- Their parents may not have a job.

- The family may not have a house.

a) How do you feel about this injustice?

_____

_____

b) What would you like to do about this situation?

_____

_____

c) What would you say to someone who is living on the streets?

_____

_____

d) Find out and note down one of the things that is being done to help children forced to live on the streets.

_____

_____

6 There are many global injustices at the moment. Here are some of them:

- Some people do not have clean water to drink.

- Some people are hungry.

- Some people have to work in very poor conditions.

- Some people do not have access to medicine.

Choose one of these and find out about it. Note down some key points here.

- _____

- _____

- _____

- _____

7 How does injustice make you feel? Describe your emotions in the diagram below.

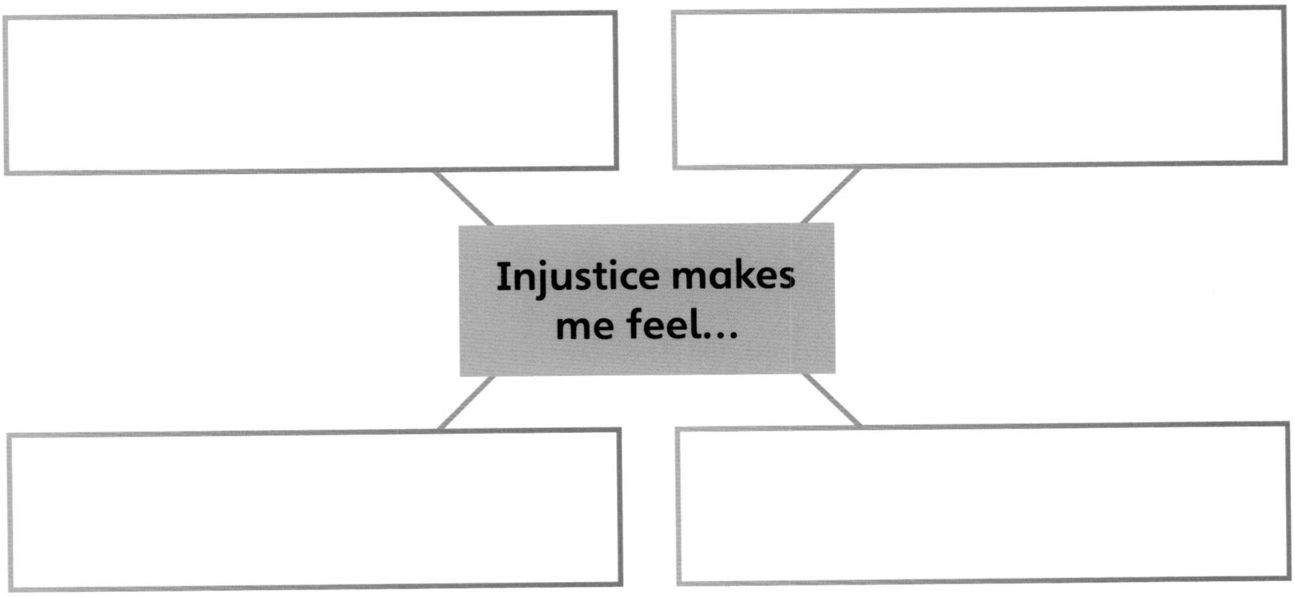

Injustice makes me feel...

8 Below are listed some International Days that highlight injustices. After research, draw lines to show the dates on which each is celebrated.

International Day of Non-Violence	12 April
International Day for the Eradication of Poverty	21 March
International Day for Street Children	2 October
International Day for the Elimination of Racial Discrimination	17 October

Choose one of these International Days and, in the box below, design your own logo for it. The pictures might give you some ideas.

9 How can you make the world a better place? What would you like to change?

Write down four ideas. Think about injustice in your school, community, country and the world.

1 _____

2 _____

3 _____

4 _____

What new things have you learned?

What had you not thought about before?

Wealth and poverty in society

Objective

SJE4.IB – Be aware of what people need to thrive.

We will learn:

- about our basic needs
- about what we need in order to thrive.

Key vocabulary

community, needs, poverty, society, survive, thrive, wants, wealth

i We have already learned that we need food and water to survive. There are also other things which we need in order to thrive. These things can include family and friends, health and education.

I Study the pictures of the three different types of home – a static home, a detached house and a block of flats. Then answer the questions.

a) In what ways are these three homes similar?

_____

_____

_____

b) In what ways are they different?

_____

_____

_____

c) What would be the best thing about living in each of these homes?

Static home: _____

_____

Detached house: _____

_____

Block of flats: _____

_____

2 Draw in the space below what your ideal bedroom would look like.

Think about the shape of the room. What about its location? Would you like the room to be underground, in an attic or outside? How will it be decorated? Where would you keep your most precious items, your toys and your clothes?

Label your drawing to show all these features.

3   Here are some things that can help us to **thrive**. What is most important to you?

| friendship | safety | a bicycle |

| education | a new jacket | an apple |

| family | freedom | love |

Order the words, writing the most important to you at the top of the diamond, down to the least important at the bottom.

4   In the table, write what you think each word means and
then look it up in the Glossary.

I think this word means...		The definition in the Glossary is...
	wealth	
	poverty	
	society	
	needs	
	wants	
	community	

Now write a sentence that includes three of the words from
the table.

_____

_____

5 Write your own poem in which you share the things that make you thrive. The poem can be up to ten lines long and doesn't have to rhyme. Look back at Activity 3 if you need some ideas.

_____

_____

_____

_____

_____

_____

_____

_____

_____

_____

Now, draw a picture to accompany your poem.

6 Choose the correct words to complete the sentences. Only use each word once.

thrive   friends   education

food   live   quality

We need air, water and _____

to **survive**, but what does it take for us to

_____? To be the best that we can

be, we need lots more things.

Safety, somewhere to _____ and an

_____ are things that improve our

_____ of life. Our lives are made even

better by family, _____, love and a

sense of belonging.

What new things have you learned?
What had you not thought
about before?

Equality of opportunity

Objective

SJE4.IC – Understand some of the barriers to equality of opportunity now and in the past.

We will learn:

- to understand some of the current barriers to equality of opportunity
- to understand the barriers to equality of opportunity in the past.

Key vocabulary

barrier, equality, opportunity, vote

ℹ️ Many people do not have equality of opportunity to do the things they want to in life. This is happening now and it has happened throughout history. Some of the reasons or barriers that prevent people having equality of opportunity are gender, ethnicity, disability, age, poverty, ill health or beliefs. These barriers can limit people's opportunities in life, for instance their freedom, education, job opportunities and self-esteem.

1   Choose the correct words to complete these sentences about the barriers to **equality** of **opportunity**. Only use each word once.

attitude	disabled	technology

environment	equality

a)   There are many barriers to _____ of opportunity for people with disabilities.

b)   The WHO (World Health Organization) says that one of the barriers is the physical _____ . This does not cater for many people with a disability.

c)   The WHO also found that _____ is not well developed to assist people with a disability.

d)   The services needed to support the _____ are often not in place.

e)   Another **barrier** is the negative _____ from other people towards those with a disability.

2 Draw lines to match the pictures with the events.

_____

1994 – Apartheid ended in South Africa and Nelson Mandela became president.

_____

1968 – Women's strikes at a car factory led to the Equal Pay Act 1970 in the UK.

_____

2010 – The UK Equality Act made it illegal to be discriminated against because of your age.

_____

1893 – Women were given the right to **vote** in New Zealand.

Then, underneath each picture, write the barrier that has been broken down. Choose from those below. You may need to use one of them twice.

age   gender   ethnicity

3   Read the following text about Roma people in Europe. Then answer the questions on this and the opposite page.

The Roma migrated to Europe from India in the 10th century.

The Roma have often faced barriers to equality of opportunity from different people and governments all around the world. Here are some examples of this from Europe.

- Most Roma in Europe live below the poverty line.

- Anti-Roma discrimination is widespread.

- More than half of Europeans said they would not want to have a Roma person as a neighbour.

- Roma generally have a life expectancy of 10 years less than the average European.

- Roma are at high risk of living in poor-quality homes.

- Many Roma people do not finish school.

a)   Where did the Roma originally come from?

_____

b)   What do you think 'below the poverty line' means?

_____

c)   Anti-Roma discrimination means that many people treat the Roma worse than anyone else. Is this true or false?

_____

d)   What would you say to someone who said they would not want to have a neighbour who is Roma?

_____

e) What would you say to someone who said it was alright for someone to live in a poor-quality home?

_____

f) Which barriers might Roma students face at school?

_____

_____

g) Patchwork is a traditional Roma craft. Look at the picture, then find out about this craft and create a design of your own for a patchwork bedspread in the box below.

4 Write below why you think it is important that all people have equality of opportunity.

_____

_____

_____

5 Throughout the world, women do most of the farm work, but the land that they work on is mostly owned by men.

What do you think about this? Write your thoughts below.

_____

_____

_____

_____

_____

6 The picture shows the UN (United Nations) logo for Gender Equality. Design a logo to show your support for the removal of barriers to equality of opportunity. What would you need to include on your logo?

Draw your logo in the box below.

What new things have you learned?

What had you not thought about before?

Challenging injustice

Objective

SJE4.ID – Understand that is it not possible to know what a person is like inside, simply by their appearance.

We will learn:

- that you cannot know what a person is really like by looking at them
- that we should not judge anyone based on their appearance
- that other people should not make assumptions about us because of how we look.

Key vocabulary

appearance, assume, judge, personality, stereotypes

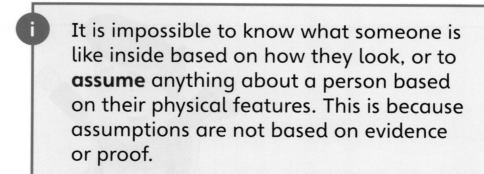

ⓘ It is impossible to know what someone is like inside based on how they look, or to **assume** anything about a person based on their physical features. This is because assumptions are not based on evidence or proof.

1 Draw a picture of yourself and then write ten words that describe your **personality**. You may need a thesaurus for this.

This is me.	These words describe my personality.
	1 _____
	2 _____
	3 _____
	4 _____
	5 _____
	6 _____
	7 _____
	8 _____
	9 _____
	10 _____

2   Different words are used to describe **appearance** and
personality. Write each adjective in the correct box in
the table.

| kind | tall | funny | athletic | thoughtful |

| short | generous | stocky | shy | friendly |

Appearance	Personality
_____	_____
_____	_____
_____	_____
_____	_____

3   How would you feel if someone judged you on your
appearance? Add words to the diagram.

I would feel...

4   Answer the following questions about **stereotypes**.

a)   Write down three examples of stereotypes that you know.

Example 1: _____

_____

Example 2: _____

_____

Example 3: _____

_____

b)   In what way are the people in your examples being stereotyped?

Example 1: _____

_____

Example 2: _____

_____

Example 3: _____

_____

c)   What could you say to someone to help them understand how damaging it can be to use stereotypes?

_____

_____

_____

5   Tick if you think the statements about stereotypes are true or false.

	True	False
Stereotyping tells us a lot about a person's personality.		
Children cannot be stereotyped.		
People are stereotyped for many different reasons.		
Stereotyping can prevent a person getting a particular job.		

6   Choose the correct word to complete each sentence. Only use each word once.

appearance   prejudice   judge

time   ignorance

a)   Stereotyping is a type of _____.

b)   We should take the _____ to get to know people.

c)   Assuming something about someone based on their

_____ is wrong. If we do this, we show our

_____.

d) 'Don't _____ a book by its cover' means that you cannot tell anything about what is inside by looking at the outside.

7 What do you think life would be like if everyone looked and acted in exactly the same way?

a) Write a short poem that describes this strange world.

Everyone's the same

_____

_____

_____

_____

_____

_____

_____

b) Would you prefer to live in the world as it really is or the strange world of your poem? Explain your choice.

_____

_____

_____

The new girl is really unfriendly. She is very quiet. She is always reading, so she will not want to join the netball team.

8   a)   **What assumptions has Hafsa made about the new girl in her school?**

_____

_____

_____

_____

b)   **Why should she rethink her opinion?**

_____

_____

_____

What new things have you learned?

What had you not thought about before?

Conflicts in the community

Objective

PC4.4A – Understand that bullying has a negative impact on both the bully and the person being bullied.

We will learn:

- that bullying can affect the person being bullied very badly
- that bullying can harm the bully, too.

Key vocabulary

cyber, online, physical, verbal

i Bullying is threatening behaviour (verbal or physical) with the aim of harming or scaring others. Bullying can harm people physically and emotionally. It is always wrong. Bullying affects both the person being bullied and the bully themselves.

I Here is a definition of bullying:

'Bullying is threatening behaviour (verbal or physical) with the aim of harming or scaring others.'

Note down any examples of bullying you can think of.

_____

_____

_____

_____

_____

_____

_____

2 How do you think being bullied makes someone feel? Add words to the diagram.

Bullying makes someone feel...

3 Choose the correct words to complete the text.
Only use each word once.

| cyber | verbal | unacceptable | hitting | spreading |

Bullying happens in many different ways. **Physical** bullying is

deliberately hurting another person by, for instance,

_____ or kicking them. Using nasty words or

_____ bullying is deeply upsetting. Anyone can be

bullied. **Online** or _____-bullying is when hurtful

messages, emails or videos are sent via the internet. Being left out

of a game or someone _____ lies about you could

lead to bullying behaviour. Whatever the type of bullying, it is

always _____.

4 What could you do if you were being bullied yourself?
Answer these questions.

a) Who could you talk to? Who would you tell?

_____

b) Where would be a safe space for you to go in your school?

_____

c) How do you think you could stop it from happening again?

_____

_____

Here are some ideas you could use to help you stand up to a bully:

- Ask them why they are doing it.

- Tell them to stop.

- Tell them you are not going to tolerate it.

- Tell them no one will like them if they behave like that.

- Tell them they would get lots of friends if they did not bully.

5   There are many reasons why a person becomes a bully. It is important to understand these reasons and the part they play in the bullying behaviour.

Complete the sentences below, giving possible reasons for the bully's feelings and imagining what the resulting behaviour might be.

a)   Aisha was jealous of Bela because _____ and so

she _____.

b)   Kim often felt lonely because _____ and so she

_____.

c)   Yusuf was unhappy because _____ and so he

_____.

d)   Miray felt embarrassed when _____ and so she

_____.

e)   Lee and his group of friends felt angry when

_____ and so they _____.

What other reasons might someone have for being a bully?
List two more reasons.

1   _____

2   _____

6   Tick all the ways you could support someone who was being bullied.

Go and speak to an adult. ☐

Ignore the person being bullied and walk away. ☐

Tell the bully to stop. ☐

Pretend it isn't happening. ☐

Get help. ☐

Tell the head teacher what you have seen. ☐

Take the person being bullied away from the situation. ☐

Don't get involved – it's not your problem. ☐

Imagine you are sitting in the school hall with your friends at lunchtime. You notice a student sitting alone, nearby, as they eat their lunch. Another student approaches them and very deliberately knocks over their glass of water. The water spills over their food and their clothes.

What could you and your friends do to support that student? Think about what you could do immediately, later that day and over the following days.

_____

_____

_____

_____

_____

7 Design a poster showing all the ways people can support someone who is being bullied. You could look at the tick list in Activity 6 for ideas, if needed.

Remember that your poster needs to make an impact – not too many words and make it as eye-catching as possible!

What new things have you learned?

What had you not thought about before?

Resolving conflicts peacefully

Objective

PC4.4B – Know how to disagree while remaining friends.

We will learn:

- how we feel when we disagree with someone
- how to stay friends even when we disagree.

Key vocabulary

compromise, conflict, resolve, respectful, solution

i You will not agree with everyone all of the time. Even the people you are closest to will have different ideas and opinions from yours. How can you disagree and stay friends? What is the solution?

1   Think about the different reasons that friends might disagree and fall out with each other.

Write your ideas in the boxes.

Friends might fall out because...

2 Draw lines to match each word with the correct definition. Look up any words you don't know in the Glossary.

conflict	To change an opinion in order to agree
compromise	An argument or disagreement
opinion	Being polite
solution	The answer to a problem
resolve	Your point of view
respectful	To find a solution to

3   How could you **resolve** these scenarios?

a)   Peter and Kwaku both want to use a yellow crayon.
There is only one. What can they do?

_____

_____

_____

b)   Mimi likes playing her music very loudly. Her sister likes peace
and quiet to do her homework. How can you resolve this
for them?

_____

_____

_____

c)   Two students want to play football. Two other students want
to play table tennis. The teacher will only allow one activity to
take place. What could you suggest they do?

_____

_____

_____

4   Choose the correct words to complete the text. Only use each word once.

listen	angry	change	feelings	frustrating
talk	shout	agree	respect	compromise

When we disagree with someone, it is easy to become _____ or upset. It is important that we recognise our _____ and think about how to respond in these situations. It might be _____ , but take a moment to consider your reaction. Even a few seconds can be enough time to _____ your response.

It is always important to give someone the chance to speak and for you to _____ to what they are saying. When it's your turn to _____ , think about what you are saying. Try not to _____ or say mean things. We don't have to _____ on everything, all of the time, but we do have to _____ someone else's right to have their own idea or opinion. Often, the solution requires _____ .

5 Think about a time you have argued or disagreed with a friend.

Write your notes below.

What did you argue about?

_____

_____

How did you feel?

_____

_____

How did they feel?

_____

_____

How did you resolve things?

_____

_____

_____

What new things have you learned?

What had you not thought about before?

Conflicts around the world

Objective

PC4.4C – Know about the Nobel Peace Prize and some of its winners.

We will learn:

- some of the history of the Nobel Peace Prize
- about some of the previous recipients of the Nobel Peace Prize
- why people have been awarded the Nobel Peace Prize.

Key vocabulary

Nobel, peace, qualities

i The Nobel Peace Prize is an award given every year to people who have been outstanding in their work for peace. Sometimes one person receives the award and sometimes it is more than one person.

1 List the names of any **Nobel Peace** Prize winners that you know.

- _____
- _____
- _____

2 Research the history of the Nobel Peace Prize online or in your library. Write down some interesting facts below.

Fact 1	Fact 2

Fact 3	Fact 4

3 Choose the correct words to complete the text. Only use each word once.

prizes	Alfred	fund

Peace	awarded

In November 1895, _____ Nobel signed his last will and testament. In it, he set up a _____ for a series of _____ in Physics, Chemistry, Medicine, Literature and _____ .

Between 1901 and 2020, the Nobel Peace Prize has been _____ 101 times to 135 Nobel Laureates: 107 individuals and 28 organisations.

4 What do you think are some of the personal **qualities** of Nobel Peace Prize winners?

Write your ideas in the boxes below.

5 What could you do to make your school more peaceful? Write your ideas below.

_____

_____

_____

6 Read this text about Ellen Johnson Sirleaf and then answer the questions on the opposite page.

Name: Ellen Johnson Sirleaf

Winner: The Nobel Peace Prize 2011 (shared with Leymah Gbowee and Tawakkol Karman)

Born: 29 October 1938, Liberia

Ellen Johnson Sirleaf became Africa's first elected female president. Her work on promoting peace, democracy and women's rights led to her being jointly awarded the Nobel Peace Prize in 2011.

Johnson Sirleaf studied at the College of West Africa in Monrovia. She moved to the United States of America in 1961 and studied economics and public policy at university. She later returned to Liberia and worked for the government there but her views led to several arguments with politicians. She was arrested twice – one sentence was for ten years.

In 2005, she ran for president and won. She brought in many improvements to living standards in the country, such as restoring the electricity supply to rural areas, reducing the amount of money (debt) owed by the country to other countries, and allowing companies and people from overseas to invest money in the country. She also won the following election which was held in 2011.

Johnson Sirleaf's work won her many honours and awards. She won the Nobel Peace Prize, along with the Presidential Medal of Freedom, in 2007. This is the highest honour that civilians (non-military) can receive in the USA and is awarded to individuals who have made improvements in world peace and a country's security and standard of living.

In which country was Ellen Johnson Sirleaf born? _____

In which year did she become president? _____

In which year did she win the Nobel Peace Prize? _____

What did she study in the United States of America?

_____

Why was she put in prison?

_____

What improvements did she bring to Liberia as president?

_____

_____

_____

What additional honour did she receive as well as
the Nobel Peace Prize?

_____

Research one more interesting fact about Ellen Johnson
Sirleaf. Write it here.

_____

_____

_____

_____

7 Here are some words that have been used to describe Nobel Peace Prize winners. They are jumbled up. Put their letters in the correct order and write the words in the boxes.

irngipsni

_____

nidk

_____

eerngsou

_____

mmiocdtet

_____

trdeemnide

_____

eecderpst

_____

cruogginnea

_____

almc

_____

kind   calm   inspiring   determined   encouraging   committed   generous   respectful

Choose one of the words and put it into a sentence about Ellen Johnson Sirleaf or another Nobel Peace Prize winner you know about.

_____

_____

_____

8 Everyone has the chance to win the Nobel Peace Prize. People win it for all sorts of reasons, but they are usually chosen for their leadership in trying to resolve serious global problems.

Think about what you would like to do in your life that might enable you to win it. Then complete the following sentences.

a) The skills I have to enable me to become a Nobel Peace Prize winner are

_____

_____

_____

b) The skills I need to improve are

_____

_____

_____

c) The global problem I would like to work on in the future is

_____

_____

_____

9 Research another Nobel Peace Prize winner and write a fact file about them.

Name: _____

Date of birth: _____

Country of birth: _____

Their job: _____

Year they won the prize: _____

Why they won the prize:

_____

_____

What they said when they won the prize:

_____

_____

Any other interesting information:

_____

_____

_____

What new things have you learned?
What had you not thought about before?

Planet Earth

Objective

SD4.7A – Know about life underwater.

We will learn:

- about creatures that live in fresh water
- about creatures that live in the oceans.

Key vocabulary

aquatic, coral reef, freshwater, habitat, invertebrates, ocean, saltwater, sea, underwater

i Planet Earth is often called the 'Blue Planet' as it is covered by so much water and looks blue from space. Underwater habitats are very diverse and are home to thousands of different creatures. Such habitats can include rivers, ponds and oceans.

1 Draw lines to match each species with its picture.

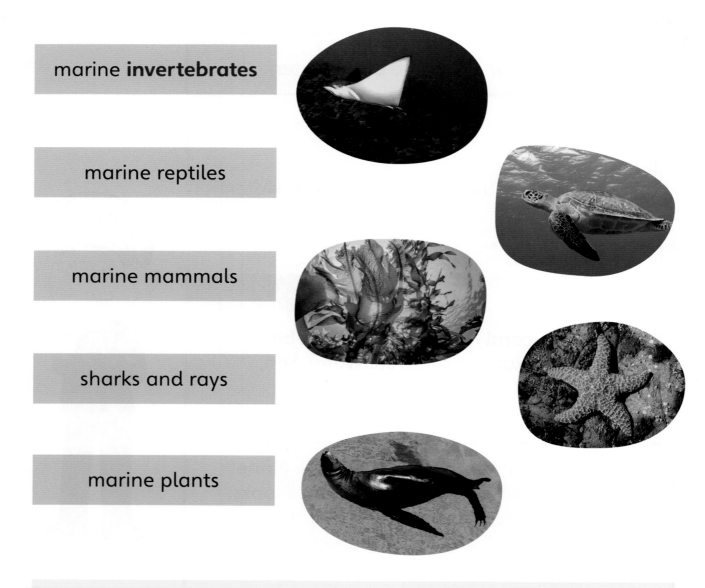

marine **invertebrates**

marine reptiles

marine mammals

sharks and rays

marine plants

2 Name all the creatures and plants that you already know that live **underwater**.

_____

_____

_____

_____

3 Read the definitions of **freshwater** and **saltwater** habitats. Then write each water habitat in the correct column of the table.

- A freshwater **habitat** has less than I per cent salt.

- A saltwater habitat has over I per cent salt.

| stream | sea | lake | river |

| pond | coral reef | canal | ocean |

Freshwater	Saltwater

4 What creatures might live in the different habitats? Write your ideas in this table.

Freshwater	Freshwater and saltwater	Saltwater

5   Choose the correct words to complete the text. Only use each word once.

eggs	habitats	snails	backbone
dolphin	fish	lakes	bottom

The freshwater _____ of rivers and lakes are home to many forms of life, from algae and _____ to insects, amphibians and fish.

Underwater, **aquatic** invertebrates are creatures that don't have a _____. Dragonflies lay their _____ on plants in the water and their larvae are fierce hunters which live under the water. Water beetles and water boatmen are insects that live in deeper water. Freshwater mussels and water snails live in the mud on the _____ of a river.

Rivers and _____ are good habitats for many types of _____. For example, Perch like slow-moving water. The Amazon River is even home to a rare and pink freshwater _____.

6 Draw lines to match each freshwater species with its description.

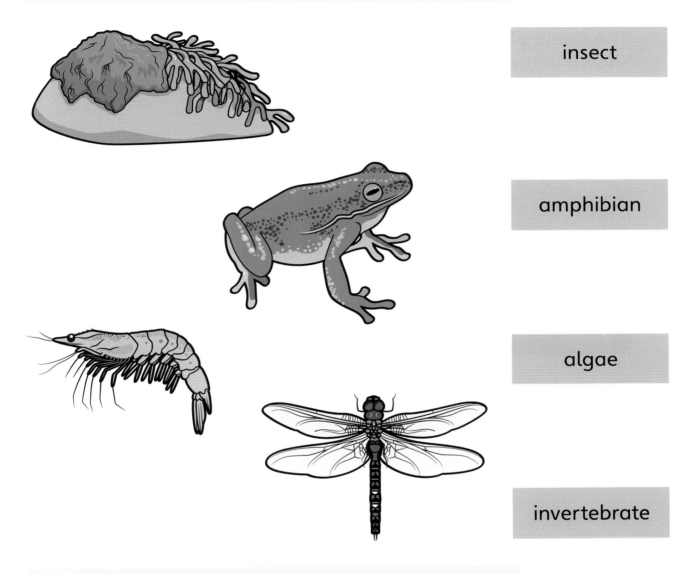

insect

amphibian

algae

invertebrate

7 What creatures and plants live in rivers and lakes in your country? Find out four facts about one of them and list these below.

1 _____

2 _____

3 _____

4 _____

8 Scientists think that 15 per cent of the world's species live in the oceans and seas.

The oceans are big places – wide and deep. The name of each of their different layers is shown in the table below. Each layer has its own specific characteristics and is home to vastly different types of creatures.

1	The Sunlight Zone (0–200m down)
2	The Twilight Zone (200–1000m down)
3	The Midnight Zone (1000–4000m down)
4	The Lower Midnight Zone (4000–6000m down)
5	The Trenches (lower than 6000m)

Research the creatures and plants listed below and tick to show which layer of the ocean they live in.

Name	1	2	3	4	5
Dolphin					
Shrimp					
Coral					
Whale					
Sea spider					
Anglerfish					
Seaweed					

9 Research one of the zones in Activity 8. Create a fact file about it and some of the species that live there. Draw one of the species in the box provided.

Fact file

What new things have you learned?

What had you not thought about before?

Connecting with nature

Objective

SD4.7B – Know how to take care of living things.

We will learn:

- how to look after seeds and plants
- what plants need to grow and be healthy
- how to take care of animals.

Key vocabulary

carbon dioxide, nutrients, photosynthesis, vivarium

i There are many ways that humans can take care of living things such as pets, plants and creatures in the natural environment. Humans have done a lot of damage to living things. If we want to continue to have the amazing variety of plants and creatures in the world, we need to think of ways that we can enable them to thrive.

1 What do living things need to grow and be healthy?
List three things.

1 _____

2 _____

3 _____

2 Complete the sentences by adding the word light, soil,
or water.

a) Most plants need _____ from the sun to grow.

b) Many plants need _____ or they will dry out and die.

c) The roots of many plants grow in _____. The plants get
the **nutrients** they need from the _____.

d) Plants need _____ and _____ to make food.

e) The **stem** transports _____ and
nutrients to all parts of the plant.

f) The leaves use a process called
photosynthesis to produce food for
the plant. They use _____, _____
and **carbon dioxide** to do this.

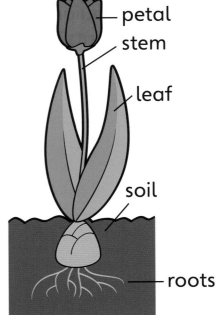

petal
stem
leaf
soil
roots

3   Read the following text about how to water plants correctly and then answer the questions.

Plants need water in order to thrive. However, there is a danger that you can over-water a plant. Plants that are directly in the ground can usually handle excess water, because there's enough area for the water to run off quickly. Plants in containers or pots though can get drowned and soggy. It is important to test the soil before watering and then only add water until the soil is 'sticky'.

a)   Why are plants in containers more likely to get over-watered than plants in the ground?

_____

_____

b)   What should you do before watering a plant?

_____

_____

c)   What equipment could you use for watering your plants? List two things.

I   _____

2   _____

4 Look at this picture of a plant. It is not healthy and thriving. Write what you think the problem might be and how you would correct it.

_____

_____

_____

5 Write the numbers 1 to 6 in the boxes to order these stages in the growth of a strawberry plant. One has been done for you.

The plant grows and begins to flower. | 5 |

Water the seeds. | |

The seeds begin to sprout. | |

Fruit grows on the plant. | |

Plant the seeds in the soil. | |

Fill a pot with soil. | |

6 Draw and label a picture to show the necessary things for taking good care of an animal. It could be your pet or any other animal you would like to look after.

7 Draw lines to match each pet with the environment it needs.

snake	Should be kept in a tank and not a bowl
cat	A hutch with straw and an outdoor run with access to grass
goldfish	Space inside and outside to roam around
rabbit	A large home, called a **vivarium**, with plenty of plants and rocks

8   How can we help wild plants and creatures?
Here is a list of things you can do.

- Plant some flowers that insects like.

- Build a wood pile in a sheltered part of an outdoor space for insects to use for shelter.

- Feed wild birds.

- Leave part of your garden wild as a shelter for creatures.

- Grow some rare plants.

- Make a pond.

Write down the ones you will be able to try.

_____

_____

_____

_____

Is there something else you would like to try?
Note it down.

_____

_____

_____

9 You are going on holiday and you have asked a friend to look after the seeds you have just sown, or your pet.

Write instructions telling them what they need to do to look after (nurture) them. Remember to tell them what they will need to use as well as what they will need to do. Make your instructions as clear as possible.

_____

_____

_____

_____

_____

_____

_____

_____

_____

_____

_____

What new things have you learned?

What had you not thought about before?

Biodiversity and habitat loss

Objective

SD4.7C – Explore rewilding.

We will learn:

- what rewilding is and where it has been successful
- the advantages of rewilding.

Key vocabulary

climate change, debate, environment, species

> **i** Rewilding is returning areas of land to an uncultivated state which can then be dedicated to nature. It is based on the idea that natural processes should be left to develop by themselves. At the same time, species of plants and animals that used to live in that environment are reintroduced to help re-establish ancient habitats.

1   Choose the correct words to complete the text. Only use each word once.

damaged	habitats	nature
wolf	beaver	struggle

Rewilding is about encouraging people to reintroduce ancient and wild _____.

This means reintroducing lost **species** and rebuilding habitats _____ by human development. Rewilding can be done in small areas, of woodland for example, or in large areas where there has been the reintroduction of native species such as the _____ and _____.

The process of rewilding can occur when _____ is left alone. It is a long-term process as species _____ to cope with the impact of human-made **climate change** on their natural habitat.

2 Across the world, different animals have been reintroduced or returned to areas where they have not lived for many years.

Draw lines to match each animal with the most appropriate country. You may need to research the animals.

Poland

Scotland

England

France

Patagonia

Indonesia

beaver

wolf

white-tailed eagle

European bison

elephant

guanaco

3 Do you think reintroducing native species of animals is a good idea? Give your reasons.

_____

_____

_____

_____

4 Do you think native species of plants should be reintroduced? Give your reasons.

_____

_____

_____

_____

5 Rewilding has led to a lot of **debate**. Some people support it and others are worried about what the impact might be.

Read the opinions below and tick the correct box. Do you think each opinion is from someone supporting rewilding or someone against rewilding?

	Support	Against
I think rewilding improves the **environment**.	☐	☐
I think it will make areas look untidy.	☐	☐
I think it will stop important building projects.	☐	☐
I would love to see some native species being given a chance to survive.	☐	☐
I think rewilding is harmful to a farmer's livestock.	☐	☐
I think it will mean that more people visit the area.	☐	☐
I think weeds will spread to land where people are growing crops.	☐	☐
I think rewilding is essential to build up biodiversity.	☐	☐

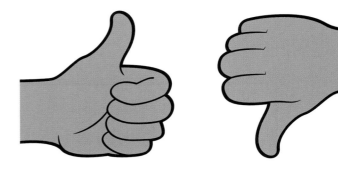

6 Look back at your answers to Activity 5. Using the opinions of those supporting rewilding, add points to the diagrams below. One diagram collects ideas to support the case for rewilding, the other for the case against it. One has been done for you.

I think rewilding improves the environment.

The case for rewilding

The case against rewilding

7 Research an animal that has benefited from rewilding and write a fact file that you could present to your class. Remember to include details about where your chosen animal lives and how its numbers have increased since rewilding. You should describe its habitat.

You could add a picture of the animal if space allows.

My chosen animal is: _____

What new things have you learned?

What had you not thought about before?

Climate change

Objective

SD4.7D – Know about climate change: what it is and some of its causes and impacts.

We will learn:

- what climate change is
- about some of the impacts of climate change
- how we can reduce the impacts of climate change.

Key vocabulary

atmosphere, carbon dioxide, climate, coal, energy, fossil fuels, gases, greenhouse gases, methane, oil, renewable, source

i Climate change is causing the weather to become much less predictable around the world. Although the climate has always changed, the climate change we are experiencing now is caused by human activity. Many people call this a climate crisis because of the enormous damage we are doing to the planet. The environmental impacts of climate change are vast, from rising sea levels to the extinction of species.

1   What do you know about **climate** change and the impact it has? Add your ideas to the diagram below.

Climate change is causing...

2   Draw lines to match the terms with their definitions. Look up any words you don't know in the Glossary.

climate change	**Gases** around planet Earth
fossil fuels	A gas formed when people and animals breathe out (exhale)
atmosphere	Extreme environmental changes caused by human behaviour
carbon dioxide	Gas, **coal** and **oil**

3   Complete the text using the correct words.

gas	underground	**greenhouse**	fossil fuels

energy	carbon dioxide	dangerous	warming

trap	atmosphere

Climate change is sometimes described as global

_____ . However, this is not very accurate because

it is not just about places getting hotter, it is about extreme

weather of all kinds. Climate change is caused by the burning of

_____ _____ which include coal, oil and

_____ . These were formed millions of years ago and

are found _____ .

When fossil fuels are used for _____ or to

power cars or factories, gases such as _____

_____ are released. When too much carbon dioxide

gets into the atmosphere, it can become _____ .

This is because carbon dioxide, **methane** and other gases form

_____ gases which _____ heat in the

_____ and warm the planet.

4 Write down a use for each of these fossil fuels.

Coal: _____

Gas: _____

Oil: _____

5 Which fossil fuel is most often used to power each of the items below? Write **coal** or **oil**.

_____

_____

_____

_____

6 a) Explain if and how you and your family use the following fossil fuels.

Oil: _____

Petrol/Diesel: _____

Gas: _____

b) What is a **renewable source** of energy? Write a definition and give two examples.

Definition: _____

_____

Example I: _____

Example 2: _____

c) Does the electricity you use come from fossil fuels or renewable sources? If you are not sure, try and find out.

_____

d) Looking at the ways you use fossil fuels at home, try and think of some ideas of how you could reduce this.

- _____

- _____

- _____

- _____

7 How do you think the use of fossil fuels could be reduced over the next ten years?

Write your ideas in the boxes below.

Locally

Nationally

Globally

8 Design a poster showing all the things you can do at home to reduce the use of fossil fuels and share it at school to inspire others. Remember, it needs to be eye-catching and the messages must be clear.

What new things have you learned?

What had you not thought about before?

Energy, pollution, waste and recycling

Objective

SD4.7E – Understand some of the causes and negative impacts of waste and pollution.

We will learn:

- what waste and pollution mean
- about some of the causes of waste and pollution
- about some of the negative effects of waste and pollution on the environment.

Key vocabulary

environment, landfill, non-renewable, pollution, recycle, reduce, reuse, waste

i Many people waste a lot of things and their behaviour causes pollution which damages the environment. Waste can include plastic, electrical goods, clothing and food. Pollution is often caused by chemicals and gases. We can all reduce the amount of waste we produce and the pollution we cause. Small adaptations to how we live can have a big impact.

1   Write your ideas in answer to the following questions.

a)   What is **waste**? What different types of waste are there?

_____

_____

_____

_____

b)   What could you do to prevent waste at home?

_____

_____

_____

_____

c)   What improvements could be made to prevent waste
at school?

_____

_____

_____

_____

d)   What is **pollution**? What different types of pollution are there?

_____

_____

_____

_____

2 Use the correct words to complete the text. Only use each word once.

electrical	food	responsible	water

landfill	clothes	consumer	gold

We are all _____ for creating different types of waste. This is having a harmful impact on our planet.

Over 30 per cent of all _____ produced is wasted or thrown away. To grow and produce food you need _____; wasting the resulting food product is also wasting precious water supplies.

Often, wearable items of _____ are thrown in the bin because we no longer want to wear them. This means they go to _____. Here, huge piles of rubbish decompose over time, releasing toxins into the air and ground, soil and harming plants and wildlife.

Waste doesn't stop there. The _____ demand for the latest technology means that large _____ items are thrown away, too. These electronics often contain valuable **non-renewable** resources such as _____, aluminium and cobalt.

3 Put each item or action into the table to show the ways in which we can tackle waste and **reduce**, **reuse** or **recycle**. Some items or actions can go in more than one category. One has been done for you.

| plastic shopping bag | batteries | yoghurt pot |

| compost food waste | egg carton | cotton nappies |

| plastic water bottle | jumper | glass bottle |

| cloth shopping bag | cardboard | travel mug |

| metal water bottle | magazines | donate to charity |

Reduce	Reuse	Recycle
	cloth shopping bag	

4 Write a sentence to explain how each of these activities causes waste or pollution.

a) Buying new trousers every week

_____

b) Buying more food than you need

_____

c) Upgrading your phone every year

_____

5 Complete the sentences to describe the impact of the following actions. What could be done instead?

a) Sending an old, but working, fridge to landfill contributes to pollution because

_____.

Instead, _____.

b) Throwing vegetable peelings in the general bin contributes to pollution because

_____.

Instead, _____.

c) Buying a plastic bag every time you go shopping contributes to pollution because

_____.

Instead, _____.

6   Answer the following questions about alternatives to plastic.

a)   What do you think people used to carry shopping in before plastic was invented?

_____

b)   What did people used to carry water in on a hot day?

_____

c)   List two things – neither of them plastic – that you could use to carry your lunch in.

_____

_____

7   How can you reduce, reuse and recycle? List your ideas about how you can minimise waste.

I can reuse:

_____

_____

I can recycle:

_____

_____

I can reduce:

_____

_____

8 Write a letter to an adult sharing your ideas about how everyone could reduce and eliminate waste in their lives to help protect the future of the **environment**.

What new things have you learned?

What had you not thought about before?

The future of our planet (Greater Depth)

Objective

SD4.7F – Know about some national or international celebration days which value our planet.

We will learn:

- that there are some specific days which highlight the value of our planet
- how we can take an active part in celebration days
- how to share our knowledge of the issues with others.

Key vocabulary

awareness, Earth Day, global citizen, international, national, participation

i There are many different national and international days of celebration for our planet. They focus on increasing awareness of sustainability, biodiversity and what we can do to protect the environment and all the life within it. Events such as Earth Day encourage **participation** and unite us in a common cause.

1   What would you like to celebrate about planet Earth? Write your ideas in the diagram.

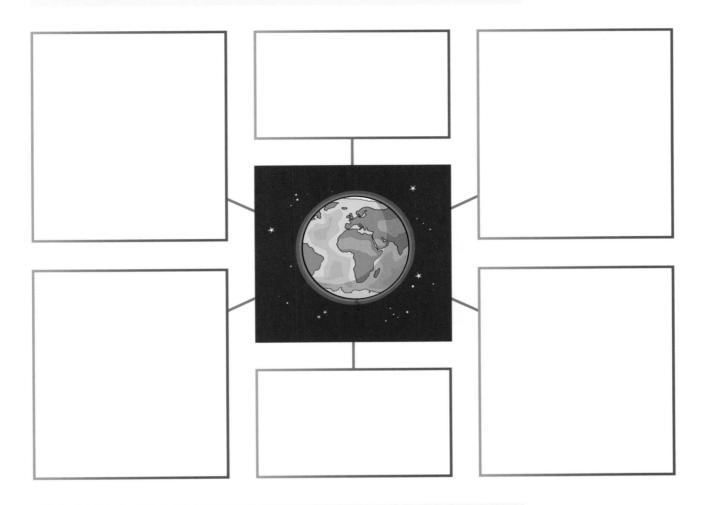

2   Choose one of your ideas from Activity 1. How could this aspect of planet Earth be celebrated? Make some notes.

- _____
- _____
- _____
- _____

3 There are many different **awareness** and celebration days that focus on our planet and the environment.

Draw lines to link the **international** or world day with the date when it occurs. You may need to do some research first.

Global Recycling Day	22 May
International Day for Biological Diversity	18 March
World Nature Conservation Day	5 June
International Day of Climate Action	24 October
World Environment Day	28 July

4 Choose one of the celebration days from Activity 3. What is it aiming to raise awareness of? How does it do this?

_____

_____

_____

_____

_____

_____

5 Read the following text about **Earth Day** and then answer the questions.

Earth Day is probably the biggest global expression of support for the environment. Events take place in more than 190 countries and the day is celebrated by more than a billion people every year. That is an astonishing achievement!

The planting of trees is a major part of the Earth Day movement and, through The Canopy Project, millions of trees have already been planted. This innovative project works to train local people in creating tree nurseries and planting out and maintaining the emerging trees. In this way, there is harmony between the local human population and the sustainability of nature.

a) What makes Earth Day the biggest celebration of planet Earth?

_____

_____

b) Why do you think the project to plant millions of trees has been called The Canopy Project?

_____

_____

c) Why is it important to involve local communities in such projects?

_____

_____

d) What other activities take place on Earth Day?

_____

6   Choose a **national** or global celebration day for planet Earth. You could look back at Activity 3 on page 96 for ideas. Make some notes about the event to share with your class.

- _____
- _____
- _____
- _____

Use your notes to design an invitation for the day. Explain what can be learned and shared through taking part in the celebration. You could use phrases like 'Discover how to...' or 'Find out about...' You might perhaps want to include questions like 'Have you ever wondered...' or 'What do you think about...'

Invitation

_____

_____

_____

_____

_____

_____

_____

7 Think about the actions you can take, as a **global citizen**, to look after planet Earth.

Write your own pledge (promise) to carry out four of these actions. Don't forget to sign and date it!

I pledge...

1 _____

_____

2 _____

_____

3 _____

_____

4 _____

_____

Signed _____ **Date** _____

8 Choose a planet Earth event that you would like to celebrate in your school. Use your own event or choose either Earth Day (information at www.earthday.org) or World Environment Day (information at www.worldenvironmentday.global).

You are going to make a game of snap to raise awareness of this event. Draw 12 pictures (or write 12 words/phrases) that represent the environmental issues highlighted by the event. For example, a picture of a whale, a chimney producing smoke, plastic waste in the sea, a rewilded meadow. Use what you have learned already in this topic.

An example of a card you might create has been done for you. Find some recycled card to make the game and play with a friend!

traffic jams			

What new things have you learned?

What had you not thought about before?

Who am I?

Objective

ID4.2A – Appreciate that our individual life circumstances make each of us unique and different.

We will learn:

- what individuality means
- what makes us unique.

Key vocabulary

individuality, unique

i There are many things that make us all unique and different. These include where we are born, which family we are born into and our own appearance, personality, interests and goals. Let's look at some of the ways we are unique and different.

1   Draw lines to match each word with its definition. Look up any words you don't know in the Glossary.

individuality	A person's nature and character
unique	Things about a person that distinguishes them from all others
personality	One of a kind

2   What things make you unique?

Draw your face and label it with six things that make you who you are!

3 Think of someone you know. Add their name to the diagram and four things about them that makes them special.

```
┌──────────────────┐        ┌──────────────────┐
│                  │        │                  │
│                  │        │                  │
└──────────────────┘        └──────────────────┘
        ┌──────────────────────────────┐
        │ My special person is _____ │
        └──────────────────────────────┘
┌──────────────────┐        ┌──────────────────┐
│                  │        │                  │
│                  │        │                  │
└──────────────────┘        └──────────────────┘
```

4 What makes us individual?
Write down the names of...

... a book that has made you think.

_____

_____

... a teacher who has helped to form your ideas.

_____

_____

... a television programme that has changed your behaviour.

_____

_____

... a friend who has had an influence on you.

_____

_____

5 Choose the correct word to complete each sentence. Only use each word once.

| same | different | unique |

| diversity | individuality |

a) We are all _____.

b) No two people are exactly the _____.

c) Our _____ makes us unique.

d) Everyone is _____.

e) _____ makes our world really

interesting.

6 Work in pairs to complete the table below with information about each other. Find your differences and similarities.

My partner	How am I different? How am I the same?
Food likes	
Food dislikes	
Other likes	
Other dislikes	
Sports/hobbies	
Eye colour	
Hair colour	

7 Read the following poem called 'Special Child' by Jacqueline Drye.

> I am a special child.
>
> I am a good and wonderful child.
>
> When I laugh, I make people happy.
>
> When I smile, I light up the room.
>
> I am smart and can do many things.
>
> One day, I'll show the world
>
> how great I am!

Now write your own version, saying all the ways you are wonderful, too.

_____

_____

_____

_____

_____

_____

Life would be much better if we were all the same!

8 Do you agree with Juan? Give reasons for your answer.

_____

_____

_____

_____

What new things have you learned?

What had you not thought about before?

Humankind: all equal; all different

Objective

ID4.2B – Learn about some great people, now and in the past, who have worked for equality.

We will learn:

- why people stand up for what they believe
- about people who have worked for equality.

Key vocabulary

boycott, inspirational, rights

i Throughout history, people have stood up for equality. Some have become a voice for those who could not speak out. These inspirational people have enabled change to happen.

1 What do you think equality means?
Write a definition.

Equality means _____

_____

2 What kinds of equality have people worked
for? Add your ideas to the diagram.

Kinds of equality

3   Choose the correct words to complete the text. Only use each word once.

ignored	defenders	treated

opportunities	equality	inspirational

Everyone should be given equal

_____. Sometimes this does

not happen. Unfortunately, there are people

whose rights are _____. There are

_____ people who speak out

on behalf of those whose voices go unheard

and stand up for people who are being

_____ unfairly. Those who take such

actions are known as rights _____.

We should all work for _____

and rights.

4 Emmeline Pankhurst was born in Manchester, England, in 1858. She worked for equal voting **rights** for women.

Emmeline formed a group called the Women's Social and Political Union, which became better known as the suffragettes.

Find out more information about Emmeline and write your notes below. Why is she an important figure?

_____

_____

_____

_____

_____

_____

_____

5 Rosa Parks is famous for being part of the Civil Rights movement in America in the 1950s. This was a time when Black people did not have the same rights as White people.

One day, on her journey to work, she refused to give up her seat on the bus to a white person. This simple act led to a year-long **boycott** of the buses in Montgomery until Black and White people were allowed to sit together on the bus.

Research Rosa Park's life and then tick to show if the statements below are true or false.

Statement	True	False
She was born in 1923.		
Before the boycott, Black people could sit anywhere on a bus.		
After refusing to give up her seat, she was arrested and fined US $10.		
She paid the fine quickly to avoid going to prison.		
After the boycott, the laws were changed to make segregation illegal.		
She was awarded the Presidential Medal of Freedom.		

6   Research someone who has worked for equality. Complete the table below with the information you find.

	What I found out about _____
When were they born?	
Where did they live?	
What did they work towards?	
How did they draw attention to these issues?	
What is the most interesting fact?	

7 Which well-known person inspires you to work for equality and to promote change? Write a letter to this person explaining what it is they have done that inspires you. Tell them what you are going to do as a result.

_____

_____

_____

_____

_____

_____

_____

_____

_____

_____

_____

What new things have you learned?

What had you not thought about before?

Challenging prejudice and discrimination

Objective

ID4.2C – Understand that stereotyping, assumptions and generalisations have power and that they can cause damage and be discriminatory.

We will learn:

- about the damage that can be caused by stereotypes, assumptions and generalisations
- that these things can lead to discrimination.

Key vocabulary

assumption, discrimination, generalisation, judge, respect, stereotype

i Our views and beliefs are shaped by what we see and read, and the influence of people around us. We need to be aware that stereotypes, generalisations and assumptions are often used by people, in books and online. We need to be able to spot and challenge these things because they are dangerous and can lead to discrimination.

1 Draw lines to match each word with its definition. Look up any words you don't know in the Glossary.

| stereotype | To think something is true all of the time when it may only be true some of the time |

| generalisation | Unjust treatment of different groups of people based on age, disability or gender |

| assumption | A mistaken belief that everyone who shares a characteristic is the same (for example, everyone who wears glasses is clever) |

| discrimination | Something that is accepted as true without proof |

2 Choose the correct words to complete the text. Only use each word once.

hurtful   individual   appearance   stereotyping

respect   everyone   judge

_____ is when we believe that all people in a particular group are the same. For example, it could be that _____ who wears glasses likes reading, or that all teenagers like to play computer games.

Stereotypes can be based on someone's ethnicity, gender or nationality and can be _____ and damaging.

It is important that we never _____ someone just because of their _____, their age, their disability or their job. We should _____ everyone as an _____.

3   What is wrong with the statements below? Add your thoughts to the table.

Statement	What is wrong with this?
Naomi, a footballer, says, "You have to be at least six feet tall and vegan to be a world-class footballer."	
Kaia, a builder, says, "Only strong men can be builders."	
Kim, a hairdresser, says, "You can only be a hairdresser if you have long hair."	
Aoife, a nurse, says, "Men can become nurses but they are not as good as women."	

4 Rewrite the sentences, changing the bold word to one of the words below so that they are no longer generalisations, assumptions or stereotypes.

some   few   many   often

sometimes   usually

a) **All** doctors are men.

_____

b) Students are **always** early for school.

_____

c) **All** scientists are experts in climate change.

_____

d) Children **always** play football.

_____

5 Circle the correct word or phrase in bold in each sentence to make it correct.

a) Stereotypes **discrimate against/favour** people.

b) **Gender/racial** stereotyping is based on someone's ethnicity.

c) Stereotyping can lead to verbal and physical **abuse/ compliments**.

d) Some crimes are motivated by **prejudice/tolerance**.

e) We should **accept/challenge** stereotyping if we see it happening.

6 Tomas and Orla are talking.

Actually, I love to play basketball and badminton.

You probably wouldn't be interested in sport because you can't play it. I'm guessing you probably spend a lot of time reading instead?

a) What assumption has Tomas made about Orla?

_____

_____

_____

b) What would you advise Orla to tell him about this assumption?

_____

_____

_____

7 Design a poster for your school explaining why stereotyping is wrong and why it can be hurtful and damaging. Remember to make your poster eye-catching, with clear messages.

What new things have you learned?

What had you not thought about before?

People and places around the world

Objective

GI4.3A – Appreciate that people around the world enjoy similar leisure activities and sharing these can enrich the lives of everyone.

We will learn:

- about the leisure activities enjoyed by people around the world
- how our leisure activities enrich our lives and connect us with others.

Key vocabulary

leisure activities, well-being

i Leisure and sport activities can improve our health and **well-being**, but they can also enrich our lives. They help us to connect with people we may not otherwise meet. It is interesting to know that similar games are played in many different places around the world.

1 What **leisure activities** do you enjoy taking part in? Add these to the diagram.

```
┌──────────────────┐        ┌──────────────────┐
│                  │        │                  │
│                  │        │                  │
│                  │        │                  │
│                  │        │                  │
│                  │        │                  │
└──────────────────┘        └──────────────────┘
          ┌─────────────────────────────┐
          │  Leisure activities I enjoy │
          └─────────────────────────────┘
┌──────────────────┐        ┌──────────────────┐
│                  │        │                  │
│                  │        │                  │
│                  │        │                  │
│                  │        │                  │
│                  │        │                  │
└──────────────────┘        └──────────────────┘
```

2 What new leisure activities would you like to try? List your ideas.

- _____
- _____
- _____
- _____

3 Choose the correct words to complete the text. Only use each word once.

sea	young	physical
outdoors	traditions	weather

Taking part in leisure activities is really important for our _____ and mental development.

Activities can take place indoors or _____ and will depend on where you live and what space you have. Outdoor activities are also dependent on the _____. If you live near the _____, there will be opportunities for a different range of leisure activities.

Some countries have leisure activities and games that are part of the _____ of that country. They have remained popular because they are enjoyed by the _____ and the old.

4 Draw lines to match each sentence with the correct activity to fill the gap.

Some children in Sri Lanka enjoy playing _____ on the beach.

kites

Flying _____ and riding bikes are popular activities in India.

Patintero

People living in places such as Colorado in the USA have lots of opportunities for hiking and mountain _____.

skiing

The cold climate in Canada means that people can enjoy skating and _____.

biking

Some children in the Philippines are inventive and play lots of games outside such as _____.

cricket

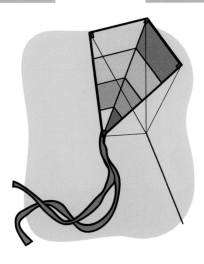

5 Read the text below and then answer the questions that follow.

> When people get involved in community activities, they may get personal rewards and feelings of achievement. As well as providing opportunities to make new friendships and connections with like-minded people, such activities offer them the chance to apply skills they already have and to develop new skills.
>
> Community activities can boost people's self-confidence and self-esteem as they learn to deal with challenges and communicate with different people.

a) Of all the benefits mentioned, which do you think is the most important? Explain your reasons.

_____

_____

b) What skills do you already have that you could use when helping with a community street party?

_____

_____

_____

c)   What new skills would you like to learn by
     taking part in a community activity?

_____

_____

_____

6 Complete each box with an activity that you are interested in and explain how it can help you do the following:

Meet new people	Being part of a community
_____ _____ _____	_____ _____ _____
Share interests	**Learn new skills**
_____ _____ _____	_____ _____ _____
Make new friends	**Improve skills**
_____ _____ _____	_____ _____ _____

What new things have you learned?

What had you not thought about before?

Global trade, ethics, production and consumption

Objective

GI4.3B – Consider the working conditions of people who provide products for us and show an interest in their well-being.

We will learn:

- about fair trade
- about the working conditions of some people who make products for us and the impact of cheap goods on workers
- how we can improve the lives of others with the choices we make.

Key vocabulary

consumers, ethical, exploited, fair trade, sweatshop

i Shops and markets are full of products that we can buy. However, if we look at the working conditions of those who make these products, we might find them less attractive. There are some ethical businesses, where the working conditions of people are of a high standard. If we want to make ethical choices, we need to know about who is making the products we are buying.

1 Find out the names of some of the companies that make the clothes you wear or grow the food you eat. In which countries are they located? Add these details to the diagram below. You may have to look on labels and packaging for this information.

Where is it made?

2 Choose the correct words to complete the text. Only use each word once.

conditions   fair   money

clean   support   countries

Buying fair-trade food means paying a _____ price for

items. Farmers receive more _____ for the crops that they

grow. This improves their working _____ and the lives of

their families. In addition, money is used to _____ local

communities and local projects such as sourcing _____ water.

The World Fair Trade Organization helps over 1.7 million farmers in

over 70 _____ around the world.

3 There are many ways that we, as **consumers**, can make sure that we do not support poor working conditions. The main way to do this is by choosing products from **ethical** companies who treat workers with respect and dignity and pay them fairly. The **fair trade** movement ensures this.

Research four items that are sold under fair trading and add information about them in each box.

_____

_____

_____

_____

_____

_____

_____

_____

_____

_____

_____

_____

_____

_____

_____

_____

_____

_____

_____

_____

4 Add words to their definitions, choosing from the words below.

ethics	working conditions	trade

global	sustainability

a) _____ : Something relating to the whole world

b) _____ : How and where someone has to work

c) _____ : A set of moral principles that we follow to be fair

d) _____ : Using resources in a way that ensures they will be available in the future

e) _____ : The buying and selling of goods or services

5 Read the text and then answer the questions.

One product that is often mined in dangerous conditions is gold. Gold mines can be hazardous places, with miners working in unsafe pits, without protective clothes. Harmful chemicals such as mercury are used in the process. This can lead to health problems and can contaminate local water supplies.

a) What are conditions like in some gold mines?

_____

b) What would you be worried about most if you were a gold miner?

_____

_____

6 Read the text and then answer the questions.

There are some fair trade gold mines where workers' rights are protected. Fair trade gold is only from mines which meet the internationally recognised Fair Trade Gold Standard. The Fair Trade Gold Standard includes strict requirements on working conditions, health and safety, handling chemicals, women's rights, child labour and protection of the environment including water sources and forests.

a) In what ways is the fair trade gold mine a safer place to work than the mine described in Activity 5?

_____

_____

b) How are women and children protected?

_____

_____

c) Why aren't all gold mines fair trade?

_____

_____

7 Because people demand cheap products, workers often have to work in harsh and unsafe conditions. What people pay for the product is not the real cost. The real cost is the effect on the workers' lives.

Choose the correct words to complete the text. Only use each word once.

exploited	daylight	factories
unsafe	sold	toys

Sweatshops are _____ where people work long hours for very low wages. Conditions inside these places are _____ and workers may have little or no access to fresh air or _____. Often, it is children who are _____ in this way. Some 250 million children below the age of 14 are forced to work in appalling conditions.

It's not just clothes that are produced in these factories. Food, _____ and electronics are, too. These are all then _____ around the world.

8 Think about what you could do to make the world a fairer place. What would you want to change? How would you go about it?

Write your mission statement, explaining your thoughts, in the box below. Design and include a logo to support your mission.

What new things have you learned?

What had you not thought about before?

Global wealth and poverty

Objective

GI4.3C – Understand what poverty is and some of its causes.

We will learn:

- about poverty
- some of the causes of poverty
- that poverty is a global problem.

Key vocabulary

ethical, governments, medicine, natural disaster, poverty, shelter, support, wars, wealthy

i

Poverty is a problem all over the world, in every country. Even rich countries have people living in poverty. Poverty is not having enough to live in a dignified, safe and contented way. People living in poverty have very few choices and there are a number of causes.

1   What do you understand about poverty?

_____

_____

_____

_____

2   Choose the correct words to complete the text. Only use each word once.

governments	access	medicine
food	**job**	**school**

There are many things that some people take for granted: for

example, _____, having possessions and going to

_____. Many people can go to a doctor if they are

unwell and get _____ to make them feel better.

People can earn money if they have a _____.

Some _____ help to **support** those that cannot

look after themselves. However, some people living in **poverty**

do not have _____ to medicine, **shelter** and

government support.

3 Complete the sentences. Then draw lines to match the pictures to your sentences.

Many people who do not have all of these things could be living in poverty.

People need to work because...

_____

_____

_____

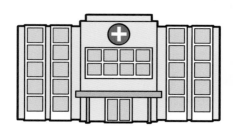

People need shelter because...

_____

_____

_____

People need medicine because...

_____

_____

_____

People need food because...

_____

_____

_____

4 What do you think causes poverty?
Write four ideas in the diagram.

```
┌─────────────────┐        ┌─────────────────┐
│                 │        │                 │
│                 │        │                 │
│                 │        │                 │
└─────────────────┘        └─────────────────┘
          ┌──────────────────────┐
          │  causes of poverty   │
          └──────────────────────┘
┌─────────────────┐        ┌─────────────────┐
│                 │        │                 │
│                 │        │                 │
│                 │        │                 │
└─────────────────┘        └─────────────────┘
```

5 Tick to show if these statements about the causes of poverty are True or False.

Statement	True	False
Natural disasters usually leave houses and shops undamaged.		
People who work are always paid enough money to buy what they need.		
Only **wealthy** people are affected by **wars** and natural disasters.		
Sometimes students cannot go to school because they have to work.		

6 Tick the actions that you think might be helpful in reducing global poverty.

Supporting **ethical** businesses ☐

Buying clothes from companies that don't pay their workers enough ☐

Not finding out how things are produced ☐

Choosing fair trade goods ☐

Only taking our fair share ☐

Buying only things we need ☐

7 A famous footballer has spoken out on behalf of families struggling with poverty. He called on the government to provide a free meal a day for students who need it. What message would you send to the footballer about what he has done?

_____

_____

_____

8 Find out about a problem caused by poverty that you would like to draw attention to. It could be a local, national or international problem. Who do you think could help solve the problem? What would you want them to do? Write your ideas below.

The problem: _____

_____

The people/organisations that can help:

_____

_____

The solution: _____

_____

_____

_____

9   How could we all help to reduce poverty in the world? Design a poster to share your ideas. Remember to make it eye-catching, with clear messages.

What new things have you learned?

What had you not thought about before?

Information, technology and communication

Objective

GI4.3D – Know some of the benefits of digital global communication.

We will learn:

- about different kinds of digital technology
- how we use this technology
- some of the benefits of digital global communication.

Key vocabulary

access, blog, communication, digital, email, internet, network, social media, technology, video, vlog, website

i Many people now use digital communications every day, either at home, at work or at school. Global digital communication has great benefits, although not everyone has access to it.

1 What kinds of **digital** communication do you use? Add your answers to the diagram.

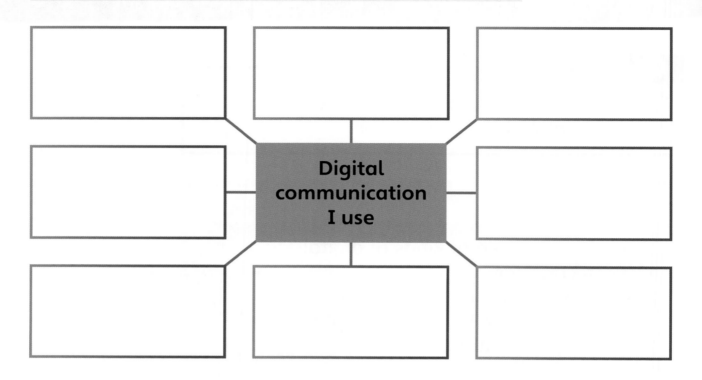

2 Write your thoughts about how digital communication impacts your life below.

_____

_____

_____

_____

_____

_____

_____

_____

3 Draw lines to match each type of digital **communication** with its description. Look up any words you don't know in the Glossary.

email	A **website** or **social media** account with regularly updated **video** content
text message	A message sent by one computer user to another via a **network**
blog	A way of seeing and hearing the people you are talking to
vlog	An informal and regularly updated website
video calling	Electronic communication sent and received by phone

4 Decide whether each of these scenarios is a positive or negative effect of having access to the **internet**. Circle **POSITIVE** or **NEGATIVE**.

I   Your grandparents live in another country. You have video calls with them every week and on special occasions.

POSITIVE / NEGATIVE

2   Someone you have been playing an online sports game with is making fun of you and calling you names.

POSITIVE / NEGATIVE

3   You have a class project to work on about endangered animals.

POSITIVE / NEGATIVE

4   You are going on a school trip and need some new clothes but the nearest shop does not have your size.

POSITIVE / NEGATIVE

5　Choose the correct words to complete the text. Only use each word once.

study	education	world

learning	**technology**	remotely

One area that is really benefiting from digital communication is _____. The _____ available in your home and school allows you to **access** so much knowledge and support to help you with your _____. People who live in rural areas and isolated places can _____ educational courses _____. Digital communication makes education available to you wherever you are in the _____.

6 As the Covid-19 pandemic took hold around the world in 2020, workplaces and schools were forced to close.

Think about how digital technology could help in this situation or what may be its disadvantages.

Write your ideas in the boxes below.

How digital technology could help

Why digital technology may not help

7 There are many benefits to digital technology for communication. Write examples of these in the table below, for the different people listed.

Person	Benefits
Student	• _____ • _____ • _____ • _____
A person living alone	• _____ • _____ • _____ • _____
Busy working parent	• _____ • _____ • _____ • _____

What new things have you learned?

What had you not thought about before?

Global health, food and well-being

Objective

GI4.3E – Know about some different types of farms and food production.

We will learn:

- about different types of farming and food production
- the advantages and disadvantages of some types of farming
- what it is we value about different farming techniques.

Key vocabulary

arable, crop, cultivation, free-range, intensive, monoculture, organic, pastoral, sustainable

i The food we eat can come from all over the world. Understanding how food is grown or animals are reared is important and we need to find out more. The global farming industry has to continually adapt and change in response to growing demand, consumer preferences and climate change.

1 Think about the food that you have eaten today. List some items. Which countries did they come from? You may have to look at labels and packaging for information.

- _____

- _____

- _____

2 Choose one of these foods and research your answers to the questions.

Chosen food_____
Where did it come from originally? _____
Where does it grow now? _____
How does it grow? _____

3 Draw lines to match each type of farming with its definition.

intensive	Growing crops such as barley or wheat
arable	Animals and crops raised using chemicals and machines
pastoral	Raising animals such as cows or sheep

4 Decide whether each of these is arable or pastoral farming. Circle the correct answer.

| arable | arable | arable |
| pastoral | pastoral | pastoral |

5 Choose the correct word to complete each sentence. Only use each word once.

range   single   farmers   **organic**   **sustainable**

a) **Monoculture** is the **cultivation** of a

_____ **crop** in one area.

b) Free- _____ farming means that animals are allowed to roam freely for all or at least part of the day.

c) _____ farming limits the use of artificial pesticides and fertilisers.

d) _____ fisheries ensure that the number of fish caught never exceeds the number being born.

e) Nomadic _____ herd their animals to find new pastures.

6 Choose one of the following farming methods and find out about its advantages and disadvantages. Make notes in the table.

monoculture   **free-range farming**   **sustainable fishery**

Farming method:	
Advantages	**Disadvantages**

7 What different types of farming and production methods are used to produce the food in a supermarket?

_____

_____

_____

_____

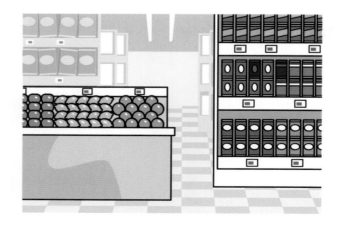

8 Here is an organic farmer. In order to make more money, she needs to change the way she farms. In order to save the environment she needs to continue with the same way of farming. What do you think the farmer should do? Give reasons for your answer.

_____

_____

_____

_____

_____

_____

I could increase my crop but it would mean using artificial pesticides, cutting down trees in my fields and always growing the same crop. However, I would make more money!

9 What do you think is the best type of farming? Why? Write the reasons for your choice in the thought bubbles.

What new things have you learned?

What had you not thought about before?

Understanding rights

Objective

HR4.5A – Understand that all children have rights that are universal and unconditional.

We will learn:

- that all children have rights which cannot be taken away
- about some children's rights.

Key vocabulary

convention, health, irrefutable, rights, unconditional, universal

i The United Nations Convention on the Rights of the Child (UNCRC) says that children – no matter where they live or where they were born – have rights. Almost all countries throughout the world have signed this agreement. The UNCRC sets out 54 rights which cannot be taken away from children. Let's look at some of these rights.

I What rights do you have? Add any that you can remember to the diagram.

My rights

2 Draw lines to match each word with its definition. Look up any words you don't know in the Glossary.

universal	Not limited in any way
rights	Cannot be argued against or denied
unconditional	Something that you are allowed to do or have
irrefutable	For everyone, anywhere

3 Complete the text with the correct words. Only use each word once.

world	Child	celebrated	Nations

protected	discriminated	heard	**health**

Since 1954, World Children's Day has been _____ on 20 November each year. It promotes international togetherness, awareness among children worldwide and improvement of children's welfare around the _____.

20 November marks two important events in history, when the United _____ adopted the Declaration of the Rights of the Child in 1959 and the **Convention** on the Rights of the _____ 30 years later in 1989.

The Convention outlines children's rights, including the right to life, _____, education and play. Additionally, every child has the right to family life, to be _____ from violence, not to be _____ against and to have their views _____.

4 Here are some examples of the rights that children have. Find out more about them. Write an explanation below and draw pictures to represent them.

Article 13: 'Freedom of expression'

_____

_____

_____

Article 16: 'The right to privacy'

_____

_____

_____

Article 19: 'Protection from abuse and neglect'

_____

_____

_____

Article 31: 'Leisure, play and cultural activities'

_____

_____

_____

5 Read Fouad's story below and put a tick beside the rights that Fouad can now enjoy.

Fouad's mum died when he was nine months old. He was then left with his unwell grandparents and his father. They had no option but to flee their home town due to the dangers of war.

Fouad's birth was never registered and, without the necessary documents, he was turned away from school. By the age of six, Fouad hadn't learned to speak.

Save the Children supported Fouad's family, who now live in another country, covering the costs of sending him to school. Today, Fouad can speak and is learning the alphabet. He says, "I like to go to school. I learn to write. I have a notebook. I can scribble."

health ☐

education ☐

play ☐

family ☐

safety ☐

6 The UNICEF book *For Every Child* begins with:

"Whoever we are, wherever we live, these rights belong to all children under the sun and the moon and the stars, whether we live in cities or towns or villages, or in mountains or valleys or deserts or forests or jungles. Anywhere and everywhere in the big, wide world, these are the rights of every child."

Use these words and all you have learned about children's rights to write your own poem celebrating the rights of the child. The title of the poem is 'Every child'.

Remember that your poem does not have to rhyme. For added impact, you could start each line in the same way: for example, with the phrase 'Anywhere and everywhere...'

Every child

_____

_____

_____

_____

_____

_____

_____

_____

7 Kavya and Nivaan are having a discussion. Kavya says that every child's rights are different and should vary depending on where they live. Nivaan says that every child has rights, whatever their ethnicity, gender, language, abilities or any other status.

a) Who do you agree with and why?

_____

_____

_____

b) What would you say to try and persuade the other person to change their opinion?

_____

_____

_____

What new things have you learned?

What had you not thought about before?

Violation of rights

Objective

HR4.5B – Be able to recognise and discuss some of the situations in which some children have their rights denied.

We will learn:

- how some children's rights can be denied
- why some children's rights might be denied.

Key vocabulary

contravene, convention, violation

i Millions of children around the world enjoy their rights because their country has signed the United Nations Convention on the Rights of the Child (UNCRC). However, even in some of these countries, children can be denied their rights. There are a lot of different reasons why this happens, but in all cases it is wrong.

1 Think about how you would feel in the following situations. Write your thoughts in the table.

Not allowed to...	Would make you feel...
play with your friends	
go to school	
see your family	

2 Draw lines to match the words with the correct definitions. Look up any words you don't know in the Glossary.

contravene	An agreement between countries
deny	To break a law or agreement
convention	Refuse to give

3 Choose the correct word to complete each sentence about children's rights. Only use each word once.

| education | life | play |

| views | healthy | safety |

a) Every child has the right to live their

_____, just as you do.

b) Every child has the right to be _____, and have access to nutritious food and clean water and air.

c) All children have the right to an _____, to improve their job prospects and living situation.

d) Children should not be forced to work; they should have the freedom to _____.

e) Many children grow up in war zones or live with the threat of violence; all have the right to _____.

f) A child has the right for their _____ to be heard; they should never be ignored.

4 The following scenarios give some reasons why a child's rights might be denied.

In each case, explain which right is being denied and why.

a) Sasha has to go to work instead of school because her parents are too sick to work themselves.

_____

_____

_____

b) Emmanuel cannot play football with his friends because he has to look after his younger brother and sister.

_____

_____

_____

c) Rudra is living in temporary accommodation because war has broken out in his town.

_____

_____

_____

5 Forced labour is one reason why some children have their rights denied. Children can be made to work on farms, in factories, on building sites, in mines, in hotels and bars, and in private homes.

Write a letter to someone who is forcing a child to work in this way, giving all the reasons why it is wrong and should stop.

Remember to use formal language, with no slang.

Dear Employer,

_____

_____

_____

_____

_____

_____

_____

_____

_____

Yours faithfully,

_____

6 Tick to show if these statements about a child's right to education are True or False. You may need to do some research first.

Statement	True	False
The United Nations Convention on the Rights of the Child (UNCRC) states that all primary-aged children must go to school.		
The UNCRC states that parents must always pay for their child's education.		
Globally, there are not many children who do not go to school.		
Of those children who do not go to school, over half are girls.		
The UNCRC states that it is not the purpose of education to prepare children for the real world.		

7 Sometimes schools are built on dangerous grounds, like near a volcano; or with materials that can cause sickness, like asbestos. Governments often do not have the money to relocate the students or rebuild the schools.

By continuing to go to school, despite these dangers, which rights of these students are being denied?

- _____

- _____

What new things have you learned?

What had you not thought about before?

Refugees, asylum seekers and internally displaced people

Objective

HR4.5C – Know that some people are forced to leave their homes and move to a place where their rights to be safe and healthy are protected.

We will learn:

- why some people might be forced to leave their homes
- that some people have to move to a different place to find safety, and this can sometimes be difficult
- what a refugee is.

Key vocabulary

natural disaster, persecution, refugee, war

i There are lots of different situations which cause people to have to leave their homes or even their country and find safety elsewhere. These can include wars, natural disasters and persecution. If people have to leave their country, they are called **refugees**. There are many examples of famous and brilliant people who are refugees.

1 Think about the different reasons why someone might be forced to leave their home. Write your ideas in the boxes.

┌─────────────────────┐   ┌─────────────────────┐
│   │   │   │
│   │   │   │
│   │   │   │
│   │   │   │
│   │   │   │
└─────────────────────┘   └─────────────────────┘

People might be forced to leave their home because...

┌─────────────────────┐   ┌─────────────────────┐
│   │   │   │
│   │   │   │
│   │   │   │
│   │   │   │
│   │   │   │
└─────────────────────┘   └─────────────────────┘

2 Draw lines to match the words with the correct definitions. Look up any words you don't know in the Glossary.

persecution	A flood, earthquake or hurricane that causes damage
natural disaster	Fighting between different countries or groups
war	Unfair or cruel treatment

3 If you had to leave your home really quickly, what three things would you want to take with you and why? Some of them may be the pictures below.

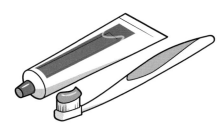

1 _____

2 _____

3 _____

4 Read the following information about Albert Einstein's life and answer the questions.

> Albert Einstein was born 14 March 1879 in Ulm, Germany. He grew up in Munich, where his father founded an electrical engineering company. After studying at university, Einstein worked at the patent office in Bern, where he produced several pioneering works in the field of physics. He was later employed at universities in Bern, Zurich, Prague and, from 1914, Berlin. He is widely considered to be one of the most brilliant men who has ever lived. However, he had to leave his home country because of persecution. In 1933, after the Nazis seized power in Germany, Einstein emigrated to the USA, where he worked at the Institute for Advanced Study in Princeton, New Jersey. Einstein won the 1921 Nobel Prize in Physics. He died on 18 April 1955.

a) When was Albert Einstein born? _____

b) In which country was he born? _____

c) At which universities did Einstein work? _____

_____

d) In which subject was he particularly skilled? _____

e) When did he move to the USA? _____

f) In which year did he win the Nobel Prize for physics? _____

5 Choose the correct words to complete the text. Only use each word once.

dangerous	scared	quickly	drought
family	disasters	change	hurricanes
disease	famine

People become refugees because they are _____ to stay in their own country. It could be _____ to stay because of war. When people have to leave their homes, they often have to leave _____ and with very few of their personal belongings. They may even have to leave _____ members behind.

Climate _____ and natural _____ have led to people seeking a new country to call home. Flooding, _____ and other extreme weather can destroy homes and huge areas of land, making places unsafe and uninhabitable owing to destruction and _____. Long periods of hot weather can cause _____ and prevent crops from growing; this causes a _____, when there is not enough food to feed everyone.

6 Here are two different people, each of whom had to leave their home and country to seek safety elsewhere.

Research their names and write in the space below the reason they had to leave their homes.

a) Malala Yousafzai, Pakistan

_____

_____

_____

b) Judith Kerr, Germany

_____

_____

_____

7 Imagine that a family has just moved in next door to you, having had to flee their home country. Write down your ideas for each of the following questions.

a) Why is it important to support this family and to help them feel welcome and safe?

_____

_____

b) What things could you and your family do to make them feel a part of their new community?

_____

_____

_____

c) What could the school do to help the children settle in quickly?

_____

_____

_____

What new things have you learned?

What had you not thought about before?

Rights defenders

Objective

HR4.5D – Be familiar with a range of people who have stood up for the rights of others both in the past and now.

We will learn:

- why people stand up for the rights of others
- about some people around the world who have defended the rights of others.

Key vocabulary

campaign, equality, law, movements, rights defender, United Nations

i A rights defender acts to promote or protect rights. Anyone can be a rights defender – all it takes is for someone to stand up for those who need their support and cannot speak out for themselves.

1   Think of some words you might use to
    describe a **rights defender**. Write these
    adjectives in the boxes below.

2   How have rights defenders made the
    world a better place? Add your ideas to
    the diagram.

Rights defenders have...

3 Choose the correct word to complete the definitions.
Only use each word once.

equality	same	others	government
organisation	positive	protect	misuse

a) Rights defender: Someone who believes in justice and

_____ and works and protests to make

_____ changes

b) **Law**: A _____ rule

c) **United Nations**: International _____ aiming to

solve the world's problems

d) **Equality**: The right of people to receive the _____

opportunities as _____

e) Defend: _____ something or someone from

_____ or harm

4 What would a rights defender do in the following situations? Complete the sentences by adding your ideas.

a) A girl pushes a younger child over and takes her sweets.

A rights defender would _____

_____.

b) A boy in the class is calling a new student horrible names.

A rights defender would _____

_____.

c) An elderly person needs help with their shopping.

A rights defender would _____

_____.

5 Why is it important for people to stand up for the rights of others? Write down your thoughts.

_____

_____

_____

6 Draw lines to match each rights defender with their cause.

Oskar Schindler (1908–1974)	Fought for Indian independence and became an inspiration for **movements** of non-violence, civil rights and freedom across the world
Rosa Parks (1913–2005)	Started an international youth movement against climate change
Mahatma Gandhi (1869–1948)	Campaigns for girls' right to education
Greta Thunberg (2003–)	Refused to give up her seat on a bus to a white man, leading to the demand for civil rights
Malala Yousafzai (1997–)	Rescued more than 1000 Jews from deportation to Auschwitz during the Second World War

7 Think about how you could be a rights defender. What right would you seek to protect? What cause would you **campaign** for? How would you go about it?

Write your action plan below.

_____

_____

_____

_____

_____

_____

_____

_____

_____

_____

_____

_____

_____

_____

8 Find out about a person who has stood up for rights. You can choose your own or one of the following:

- James Baldwin

- Janusz Korczak

- Eglantyne Jebb

Then present your information as a fact file.

Rights defender fact file

Name of rights defender:
_____

_____

The right they protected:
_____

_____

The action they took:
_____

_____

_____

_____

Result of their action:
_____

What new things have you learned?
What had you not thought about before?

Good governance (Greater Depth)

Objective

PG4.6A – Know and experience how to help to make changes for the better in school.

We will learn:

- about activities that can be done by a school council
- how to make positive changes in school.

Key vocabulary

candidate, council, elects, mission statement, policies, represents, representatives, vote

i There are many ways that changes can be made for the better in school. School councils are one way to hear the views and opinions of the whole school community. An effective school council has excellent representatives. Let's consider some of the qualities of a good school council member. Perhaps you would like to be one!

1 What changes would you like to make in your school? Add your ideas to the diagram.

possible changes

2 Do you have a school **council**? Look at the box that applies to you and follow the instructions.

YES	**NO**
Find out who is in charge of your school council and how your class is represented.	Find out how a school council works.

3 Choose the correct words to complete the text. Only use each word once.

opinions	meet	**elects**	council	reps

campaigns	visitors	planned	lead	**policies**

A school _____ **represents** the views and _____ of all students in school. Each class in each year _____ one or two **representatives** – sometimes called _____ – to speak on their behalf. Representatives _____ on a regular basis with the head teacher and other adults in the school to discuss issues affecting school life.

Students' views are considered when _____ and projects to support learning or fundraising for new equipment or facilities are _____. Sometimes the student council will represent the school when there are _____ or will attend events off the school premises. School councils will often _____ on whole-school celebrations for local or national festivals. They will also promote school _____ such as anti-bullying or improving the school's environment.

A **mission statement** outlines the purpose or goal of an organisation. These are some examples:

Our student council wants to promote projects that protect our environment.	Our student council wants to build links with local businesses and organisations.

Write a mission statement for your school council.

_____

_____

_____

_____

_____

_____

_____

_____

_____

_____

_____

5 What qualities does a good student council representative need? Write an idea in each thought bubble.

6   Imagine your school is holding its elections for the school council representatives. You would like to represent your class.

Design a poster for your election campaign to persuade students to **vote** for you. This should include something from your mission statement and reasons why you are a good **candidate**. Your messages need to be clear.

7 Look back at Activity 1 and choose one of your ideas. Complete the information below.

In school, I would like to change/introduce...

_____

_____

I would like this to happen because...

_____

_____

I am going to get other students' opinions by...

_____

_____

I am going to present my ideas and findings using...

_____

_____

I am going to present my ideas to...

_____

_____

What new things have you learned?

What had you not thought about before?

Participation and inclusion

Objective

PG4.6B – Understand some reasons why some people lack the power to fully participate in society.

We will learn:

- about some of the reasons that stop people fully participating in society
- some real-life examples of where people have lacked the power to fully participate in society
- how we can address our own discrimination.

Key vocabulary

authority, discrimination, participate, society

i There are a number of reasons why some people keep power for themselves and will not allow others to participate fully in society. These reasons include discrimination, fear, insecurity, a feeling of superiority and prejudice against those who do not look like them. Despite this, there are many examples of people who have overcome these barriers and made enormous contributions to society.

1 Why do some people lack the power to take part in **society**? Tick all the reasons that apply.

Some people are discriminated against. ☐

Some people are shy. ☐

Some people only give power to people who look like them. ☐

Some people in power do not want to share such power with others. ☐

Some people do not want to take part in society. ☐

Some people behave as if they are superior to others and prevent others having the same chances that they had. ☐

Some people only give power to people who went to the same school as them. ☐

a) How could you ensure that you give support to people who lack the power to take part in society?

_____

_____

_____

b) What is the first thing you are going to change about how you think about people?

_____

_____

_____

2 Read the following text and answer the questions that follow.

In 1951, Oliver Brown's daughter, Linda, was not allowed to enrol in her local all-White school in Kansas, USA. Some people in the area wanted to keep Black and White students separated. So Linda, along with 12 other Black students, had to take a much longer journey, including a bus ride, to get to the segregated all-Black school further away. Because White people had the power in Kansas, they prevented Black people being able to participate in society. This is **discrimination**. Oliver Brown worked against this discrimination and tried to get the law changed.

a) Why did some White people want to prevent Linda from attending the all-White school?

_____

_____

b) Why do you think Oliver Brown felt so strongly that his daughter should be allowed to go to the all-White school?

_____

_____

c) What would you say to Linda about her father's actions?

_____

_____

3 Read the following story and answer the questions that follow.

Once upon a time there was a greedy king who had a lot of power and did not want to give any to anyone else. He was in charge of all the money, the army and all the people.

People felt they were not being treated fairly and became very angry about the situation. Some people tried to advise the king but he wouldn't listen, and so he missed out on all the good ideas they had.

a) What are the disadvantages for people who take all the power?

_____

_____

_____

b) How do people who are not given any power to **participate** in society feel?

_____

_____

_____

c) Why do you think someone would want to have all the power to themselves?

_____

_____

_____

4 Complete the story from Activity 3 whereby the king realises his mistakes and changes his behaviour. If you have space, you could illustrate your writing.

5   Choose the correct word to complete the text. Only use each word once.

stand	discrimination	beliefs	lonely
help	support	report	scared

How do you think you would feel if you weren't allowed to go to school or play sport because of your appearance or

_____ ? Would you _____ up for

yourself or accept the situation?

Experiencing _____ can make you feel sad,

_____ , embarrassed, angry and _____ .

It may feel like there is no one to _____ you. No one should ever have to feel this way.

If you experience or see someone facing discrimination, there are some things that you can do:

- You can stand up for yourself or another person.

- You can tell the person their behaviour is not acceptable.

- You can get _____ from a trusted adult.

- You can ask an adult to _____ it to an **authority** that can provide support.

Don't ever be afraid to ask for help. It's an important life skill that will help you throughout school and the rest of your life.

6 Some people lack the power to fully participate in society because those in charge only give power to people who look like them.

Read the following text and answer the questions.

> Martha is very good at maths. She enjoys watching films and has a lot of friends. She also loves dancing and wants to be an astronaut when she grows up. She has put herself forward to be a school prefect but has not been chosen. None of the other students who were chosen to be prefects look like her.

a) Is it fair that, because Martha does not look like the other prefects, she cannot be one?

_____

_____

_____

b) What characteristics do you think Martha may have that would make her a good prefect?

_____

_____

_____

What new things have you learned?
What had you not thought about before?

access – the right to enter a place, use something, see someone

appearance – the way someone or something looks to other people

aquatic – living or growing in water

arable – relating to growing crops

assume – to think that something is true, although you do not have definite proof

assumption – something that you think is true although you have no definite proof

atmosphere – the mixture of gases that surrounds a planet

authority – the power you have because of your official position

awareness – knowledge or understanding of a particular subject, situation, or thing

barrier – a rule, problem that prevents people from doing something, or limits what they can do

blog – a web page containing information or opinions from a particular person or about a particular subject, to which new information is added regularly

boycott – to refuse to buy something, use something, or take part in something as a way of protesting

campaign – a series of actions intended to achieve a particular result relating to politics or business, or a social improvement

candidate – someone who is being considered for a job or is competing in an election

carbon dioxide – gas produced when animals breathe out, when carbon is burned in air, or when animal or vegetable substances decay

climate – the typical weather conditions in a particular area or over time

climate change – the large shifts in weather patterns, both natural and, more recently, human-produced through the emissions of greenhouse gases

coal – a hard black mineral which is dug out of the ground and burned to produce heat

communication – how people share information or express their thoughts and feelings

community – the people who live in the same area or town and/or a group of people who share something like culture, and interests

compromise – an agreement that is achieved after everyone involved accepts less than what they wanted at first, or the act of making this agreement

conflict – a state of disagreement or argument between people, groups or countries

consumers – people who buy and use products and services

contravene – to do something that is not allowed according to a law or rule

convention – a formal agreement, especially between countries, about particular rules or behaviour

coral reef – a line of hard rocks formed by coral, found in warm sea water that is not very deep

council – a group of people that are chosen to make rules, laws, or decisions, or to give advice

crop – a plant such as wheat, rice or fruit that is grown by farmers and used as food

cultivation – the preparation and use of land for growing crops

cyber – relating to computers, especially to messages and information on the internet

debate – discussion of a particular subject that often continues for a long time and in which people express different opinions

digital – using a system in which information is recorded or sent out electronically

discrimination – the practice of treating one person or group differently from another in an unfair way

elect – to choose someone for an official position by voting

Earth Day – an event happening on 22 April every year to demonstrate support for the environment

energy – power that is used to provide heat or operate machines

environment – the natural features of a place, for example its weather, the type of land it has, and the type of plants that grow in it

equality – a situation in which people have the same rights or advantages

ethical – relating to principles of what is right and wrong

exploit – to treat someone unfairly by asking them to do things for you, but giving them very little in return

fair trade – the activity of making, buying, and selling goods in a way that is morally right, for example by making sure that international labour laws are obeyed, that the environment has not been damaged by making the goods, and that the people who grow or make a product have been paid a fair price for it

fossil fuels – fuels such as coal or oil, produced by the gradual decaying of plants and animals

free-range – relating to a type of farming which allows animals such as chickens and pigs to move around and eat naturally, rather than being kept in a restricted space

freshwater – water that contains no salt

gases – substances such as air, which are not solid or liquid, and usually cannot be seen; also substances burned for heating and cooking

generalisation – a statement about all the members of a group that may be true in some or many situations but is not true in every case

global citizen – a person who places global citizenship above their national or local identity

governments – groups of people who govern a country or state

greenhouse gases – gases, especially carbon dioxide or methane, that are thought to trap heat above the Earth and cause the greenhouse effect

habitat – the natural home of a plant or animal

health – the general condition of your body and how healthy you are

individuality – the qualities that make someone or something different from other things or people

injustice – a situation in which people are treated very unfairly and not given their rights

inspiration – a good idea about what you should do, write or say, especially one which you get suddenly

intensive – involving a lot of activity, effort, or careful attention in a short period of time

international – relating to or involving more than one nation

invertebrates – living creatures that do not have a backbone

irrefutable – cannot be proved to be wrong, and must be accepted

judge – to form or give an opinion about someone or something after thinking carefully about all the information you know about them

justice – fairness in the way people are treated

landfill – the practice of burying waste under the ground, or the waste buried in this way

law – a rule for a certain country or community

leisure activities – time when you are not working or studying and can relax and do things you enjoy

medicine – a substance used for treating illness, especially a liquid you drink

methane – a gas that you cannot see or smell, which can be burned to give heat

mission statement – an official statement about the aims of a company or organisation

monoculture – the practice of growing only one single plant or crop or breeding the same livestock species in a field at a time

movement – groups of people who share the same ideas or beliefs and who work together to achieve a particular aim

national – relating or happening within one nation

natural disaster – a sudden event such as a flood, storm, or accident which causes great damage or suffering

needs – what someone needs to have in order to live a normal healthy comfortable life

network – a group of people or organisations that are connected or that work together

Nobel – one of the prizes given each year to people who have done important work in various types of activity. There are prizes for special achievements in physics, chemistry, economics, literature, and peace. The Nobel prizes were established by Alfred Nobel and are given in Sweden.

non-renewable – non-renewable types of energy such as coal or gas cannot be replaced after they have been used

nutrients – chemicals or food that provide what is needed for plants or animals to live and grow

ocean – one of the five very large areas of sea on the Earth's surface

oil – the thick dark liquid from under the ground from which petrol is produced

online – connected to other computers through the internet, or available through the internet

opportunity – a chance to do something or an occasion when it is easy for you to do something

organic – relating to farming or gardening methods of growing food without using artificial chemicals, or produced or grown by these methods

participate – to take part in an activity or event

pastoral – raising animals such as cows or sheep

peace – a situation in which there is no war or fighting

persecution – cruel or unfair treatment of someone over a period of time

personality – someone's character, especially the way they behave towards other people

photosynthesis – the production by a green plant of special substances like sugar that it uses as food, caused by the action of sunlight on chlorophyll

physical – related to someone's body rather than their mind or emotions

plankton – the very small forms of plant and animal life that live in water, especially the sea, and are eaten by fish

policies – ways of doing things that have been officially agreed and chosen by a political party, a business, or another organisation

pollution – the process of making air, water and soil dangerously dirty and not suitable for people to use, or the state of being dangerously dirty

poverty – the situation or experience of being poor

prejudice – an unreasonable dislike and distrust of people who are different from you in some way

recycle – the process of treating used objects or materials so that they can be used again

reduce – to make something smaller or less in size, amount, or price

refugee – someone who has been forced to leave their country

renewable – if an agreement or official document is renewable, you can make it continue for a further period of time after it ends

represent – to officially speak or take action for another person or group of people

representatives – people who officially speak or take action for another person or group of people

resolve – to find a satisfactory way of dealing with a problem or difficulty

respect – a feeling of admiring someone or what they do, especially because of their personal qualities, knowledge, or skills

reuse – to use something again

rights – something that you are allowed to do or have

rights defenders – people who have defended the rights of people currently and in the past

saltwater – water containing salt or living in saltwater or the sea

sea – the large area of salty water that covers much of the Earth's surface

shelter – a place to live, considered as one of the basic needs of life

social media – ways of sharing information, opinions, images or videos using the internet, especially social networking sites

society – a particular large group of people who share laws, organisations or customs

solution – a way of solving a problem or dealing with a difficult situation

source – a thing, place or activity that you get something from

species – a group of animals or plants whose members are similar and can breed together to produce young animals or plants

stereotype – a belief or idea of what a particular type of person or thing is like. Stereotypes are often unfair or untrue

support – to help someone by being sympathetic and kind to them

survive – to continue to live after an accident, war, or illness

sustainable – able to continue without causing damage to the environment

sweatshop – a small business or factory where people work hard in bad conditions for very little money – used to show disapproval

technology – new machines, equipment, and ways of doing things that are based on modern knowledge about science and computers

thrive – to become very successful or very strong and healthy

unconditional – not limited by or depending on any conditions

underwater – below the surface of an area of water, or able to be used there

unique – of which only one or very few exists; something that is rare

United Nations – an international organisation that tries to find peaceful solutions to world problems

universal – involving everyone in the world or in a particular group

verbal – relating to words or using words, not written

violation – an action that breaks a law, agreement or principle

vivarium – a place indoors where animals are kept in conditions that are as similar as possible to their natural environment

vlog – a website that has videos recorded by a particular person, that include their ideas and opinions

vote – to show which person or party you want, or whether you support a plan, by marking a piece of paper or raising your hand

wants – some things that you would like to have

war – when there is fighting between two or more countries or between opposing groups within a country, involving large numbers of soldiers and weapons

waste – when something such as money or skills or an object are not used in a way that is effective, useful, or sensible

wealth – material wealth: having a lot of money or possessions; emotional wealth: having support from family and friends and feeling valued

well-being – a feeling of being comfortable, healthy, and happy